About This Book

Welcome to *Investigating Science—Weather & Climate*! This book is one of eight must-have resource books that support the National Science Education Standards and are designed to supplement and enhance your existing science curriculum. Packed with practical cross-curricular ideas and thought-provoking reproducibles, these all-new, content-specific resource books provide intermediate teachers with a collection of innovative and fun activities for teaching thematic science units.

Included in this book:

Investigating Science—Weather & Climate contains five cross-curricular thematic units, each containing:

- Background information for the teacher
- Easy-to-implement instructions for science experiments and projects
- Student-centered activities and reproducibles
- Literature links

Cross-curricular thematic units found in this book:

- *Wind*
- *Clouds and Precipitation*
- *Storms*
- *Predicting the Weather*
- *Climate*

Other books in the intermediate Investigating Science series:

- *Investigating Science—Animals*
- *Investigating Science—Plants*
- *Investigating Science—The Earth*
- *Investigating Science—Space*
- *Investigating Science—The Human Body*
- *Investigating Science—Light & Sound*
- *Investigating Science—Energy, Magnetism, & Machines*

Wind

Hang on to your hat! These hands-on experiments and activities are going to bring a great breath of fresh air into your classroom!

Background for the Teacher

- *Wind* is moving air.
- Wind is caused by the uneven heating of the air around the earth by the sun.
- *Circulation* occurs when hot air rises and cool air flows in to replace it. Circulation over the entire earth is called *general circulation.*
- Wind carries storms from one place to another.
- Some winds, called *local winds,* are found only in certain places on the earth. *Monsoons* (seasonal winds found mainly in southern Asia that normally bring heavy rains) and *chinooks* (dry, warm winds blowing down the eastern slopes of the Rocky Mountains) are examples of local winds.
- *Wind direction* is the direction *from* which the wind is blowing. A *weather vane* detects wind direction.
- *Wind speed* is the rate of the air's motion. An *anemometer* measures wind speed.
- The *Beaufort wind scale* is a series of names and numbers that indicate wind speeds based on the observable effects of the wind.

Books for Blustery Days

Catch the Wind! All About Kites by Gail Gibbons (Little, Brown and Company; 1995)

Feel the Wind (Let's-Read-and-Find-Out Science® books) by Arthur Dorros (HarperTrophy, 1990)

Storm Warning: Tornadoes and Hurricanes by Jonathan D. Kahl (Lerner Publications Company, 1993)

When Bear Stole the Chinook: A Siksika Tale by Harriet Peck Taylor (Farrar, Straus & Giroux, Inc.; 1997)

The Windy Day by G. Brian Karas (Simon & Schuster Books for Young Readers, 1998)

Weather Vanes
(Making an Instrument, Experiment)

Keep track of the direction from which the wind blows with student-made weather vanes. Divide your class into groups of four or five students. Provide each group with the materials listed below; then guide the groups through the steps for making and using a weather vane.

Materials for each group: small length of poster board, scissors, tape, pen cap, knitting needle or chopstick, modeling clay, brick, marker, 4 cards, compass, 1 copy of page 8 for each student

Steps:
1. Cut an arrow from the poster board and tape a pen cap to its middle. Press a tiny lump of clay to the arrow point as shown.
2. Use the remaining clay to attach the knitting needle to the brick; then slide the pen top over the needle.
3. Label each card "N," "S," "E," or "W." Take the labeled cards, the compass, the tape, and the weather vane outdoors.
4. Position the vane in a large open area. (The higher the vane, the better the reading.)
5. Using the compass as a reference, tape the directional cards to the sides of the brick.
6. Record the wind direction daily on the wind tracker on page 8. Remember that the arrow on your weather vane points to the direction *from* which the wind is blowing.

From Your Friends at The MAILBOX®

Weather & Climate

Grades 4–6

INVESTIGATING SCIENCE

Project Manager:
Elizabeth H. Lindsay

Writers:
Michael Foster and Patricia Twohey

Editors:
Cayce Guiliano, Peggy Hambright, Deborah T. Kalwat,
Scott Lyons, Jennifer Munnerlyn

Art Coordinator:
Clevell Harris

Artists:
Nick Greenwood, Clevell Harris, Rob Mayworth,
Greg D. Rieves

Cover Artists:
Nick Greenwood and Kimberly Richard

www.themailbox.com

©2000 by THE EDUCATION CENTER, INC.
All rights reserved.
ISBN #1-56234-394-7

Manufactured in the United States
10 9 8 7 6 5 4 3 2

Table of Contents

Key:

Warm   Cold   Occluded   Stationary

L Low pressure area
H High pressure area

0s 10s 20s 30s 40s 50s 60s 70s 80s 90s 100s   Storms Rain   Ice   Snow

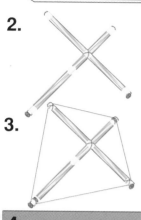

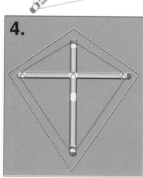

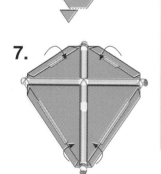

Considering Kites
(Making a Kite, Experiment)

Kites aren't just for toys! From 1898 to 1933, the U.S. Weather Bureau operated kite stations. Explain to your students that box kites with weather-measuring devices were flown from these stations. Have each student follow the directions below to make his own kite, and then take the students outside to examine firsthand just how the wind makes a kite fly. Ask students what they think makes their kites fly—is it just the wind or are there other reasons? Then point out that a kite must strike the air with greater pressure on its face than its back. This difference in pressure between the face and back then creates *lift,* the force that makes the kite rise. *Drag* is the resistance of the air to the forward motion of the kite. Lift and drag, along with line tension and gravity, keep the kite soaring.

Materials for each student: 2 sheets of newspaper, tape, string, large piece of paper, pencil, crayons or markers, scissors, kite string, fabric scraps

Steps:
1. Fold one sheet of newspaper in half. Roll it up tightly to make a pole. Tape it at both ends and in the middle. Repeat with the other piece of newspaper.
2. Use the string to tie the two poles together.
3. Beginning at one end of the poles, wrap and tape string around each end to form a kite shape.
4. Lay the kite frame on top of the large piece of paper. Trace the kite shape, making your tracing larger than the kite frame.
5. Cut out the kite shape. Cut off the four pointed corners as shown.
6. Use crayons or markers to decorate your kite.
7. Lay the kite frame on the back of the kite cutout. Fold the paper over the string on one side of the kite. Tape it down. Do this with the other three sides.
8. Use scissors to carefully punch two holes at both the top and bottom of the kite. Add kite string, as shown, and a tail with fabric scraps attached. (The more wind there is, the more tail is needed. Start with a tail at least seven times the kite's diagonal length. Then add or remove cloth strips as needed.)

A Wishing Wind
(Poetry, Writing)

Bring in a gust of creative poetry writing to your classroom by having students imagine that when the wind blows, it can bring anything one wishes for. Read a few pages from *Make Things Fly: Poems About the Wind* by Dorothy M. Kennedy (Margaret K. McElderry Books, 1998). Then tell each student to write a free verse poem about what he would want the wind to bring him. Remind students that a free verse poem has no specific form and doesn't have to rhyme. Encourage students to include devices like personification, repetition, and alliteration (for example, "The wind woke him, woke him with her whistling."). Have each student write the final copy of his poem on a simple sailboat shape cut from light-colored construction paper. Post the sailboats on a blue bulletin board titled "A Wishing Wind."

A Wishing Wind

The wind blows; make a wish!
Three seconds is all you have.
The swishing, wishing wind
Doesn't give you time to
Think.
What can you do with an
African elephant?

by Wade

Beaufort Dominoes
(Game)

		smoke rises vertically	light air

Put the Beaufort wind scale into play with this fun center game! Explain to students that since it was created in 1805, people have used Sir Francis Beaufort's scale for determining wind speeds. This scale indicates wind speeds that are based simply on observable effects. In advance, make a copy of the scale shown below. Then use a marker to divide each of 14 index cards in half so they look like dominoes. Label each domino with information from the Beaufort scale as shown at the right. (Notice each domino card is labeled with an observable effect on the left side and a description name on the right side, with the exception of two blank sides.) Then place the copy of the Beaufort scale, the dominoes, and a copy of the game directions below at a center. In turn, send student pairs to the center to play the game. If desired, program 14 additional cards in the same manner using the information in the other two columns (number and speed/MPH). Allow each pair to play this game as a second round.

smoke drifts slowly	light breeze	leaves rustle; wind felt on face	gentle breeze

leaves and small twigs move	moderate breeze	small branches move	fresh breeze

small trees sway	strong breeze	large branches sway	moderate gale

whole trees sway; difficult to walk against wind	fresh gale	twigs break off trees	strong gale

shingles blown off roof	whole gale	trees uprooted	storm

wide-spread damage	hurricane

extreme damage	

Game Directions:
1. Each player draws three dominoes. The remaining dominoes are spread facedown and become the pool.
2. Player 1 begins the game by placing one of his dominoes faceup between him and his opponent.
3. Player 2 must play a domino so that when it's placed at one end of the one already played, the information about the wind speeds matches that shown on the Beaufort scale.
4. If Player 2 cannot make a play, he draws from the pool. He can play that domino, if possible. If not, he adds it to his set. Then it's Player 1's turn again.
5. The game continues until a player plays all of his dominoes.

Beaufort Wind Scale

Number	Speed/MPH	Description	Observation
0	less than 1	calm	smoke rises vertically
1	1–3	light air	smoke drifts slowly
2	4–7	light breeze	leaves rustle; wind felt on face
3	8–12	gentle breeze	leaves and small twigs move
4	13–18	moderate breeze	small branches move
5	19–24	fresh breeze	small trees sway
6	25–31	strong breeze	large branches sway
7	32–38	moderate gale	whole trees sway; difficult to walk against wind
8	39–46	fresh gale	twigs break off trees
9	47–54	strong gale	shingles blown off roof
10	55–63	whole gale	trees uprooted
11	64–73	storm	widespread damage
12–17	74 and above	hurricane	extreme damage

Wind at Work
(Brainstorming, Research, Art)

Get your students breezing through some creative brainstorming and research. Give each student a piece of 9" x 12" light-colored construction paper. Have the student cut out a road sign of any shape and title it "Wind at Work." Tell students that wind does many things for people and in nature. Challenge each student to take a few minutes to brainstorm different ways that wind is used, such as spreading seeds, flying kites, pushing sailboats, providing power, and bringing rain. Then have each student choose one of the ideas she's listed to put on her sign. After the student comes up with a specific job that wind does, have her illustrate her wind at work (see examples). Post the signs along a wall in your classroom, adding decorative details such as those shown. Title the display "Wind at Work."

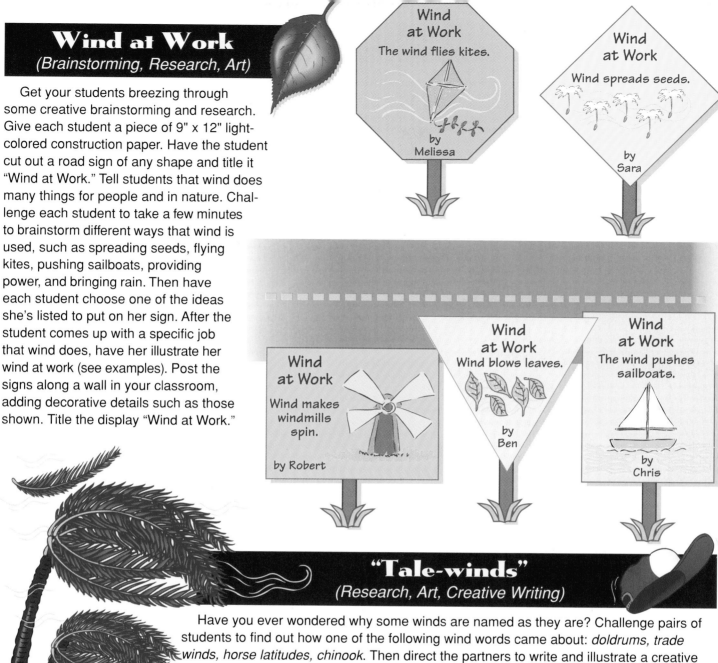

"Tale-winds"
(Research, Art, Creative Writing)

Have you ever wondered why some winds are named as they are? Challenge pairs of students to find out how one of the following wind words came about: *doldrums, trade winds, horse latitudes, chinook*. Then direct the partners to write and illustrate a creative story that tells about what they learned. Remind students to include a beginning, a middle, an ending, and character and setting descriptions. Also, encourage students to include other story devices such as dialogue. After sharing students' stories and pictures, create a display with a wind character and streamers of crepe paper representing the blowing wind. Attach students' work to each streamer (see example) and title the display "'Tale-winds.'"

Wind Tracker

Each day for a period of two weeks, use your weather vane to determine the direction of the wind. Then color one section of the bar on the kite for that direction. If on another day the wind blows from the same direction, color another section of the bar in that direction. See the sample below.

Sample
Shows the wind blowing two days from the east and four days from the southeast.

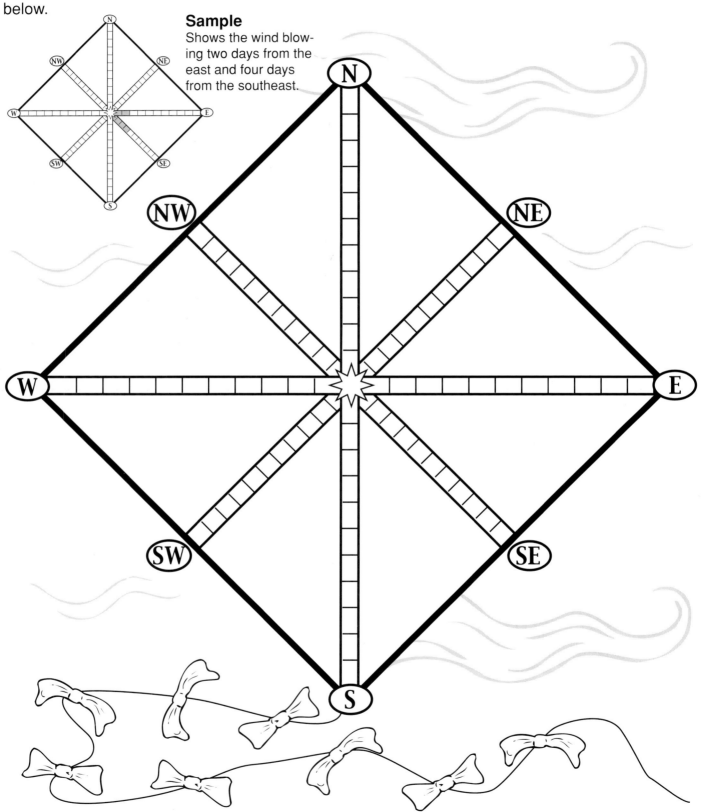

Note to the teacher: Use with "Weather Vanes" on page 4.

Name _____

The World's Winds

Learn about the world's winds by following the directions to complete the activity below.

Directions:

1. Read the paragraphs on how winds circulate on the earth.
2. Use the information in the paragraphs and the color code to color each section of the diagram.
3. Label the equator and the North and South Poles in the boxes. Then label the types of wind on the correct blanks using the following names: *polar easterlies, trade winds,* and *prevailing westerlies.*

The air of our planet is always moving. This air movement is called *general circulation.* It is caused by the uneven heating of the earth's atmosphere (as the warm air rises, surface air flows in to replace it). This warming and replacing process produces winds that tend to circle the earth in six wide bands. There are three bands in the Northern Hemisphere and three bands in the Southern Hemisphere. These six bands are called the *prevailing winds.* Because the earth rotates from west to east, the wind bands moving toward the equator seem to bend to the west and the wind bands moving away from the equator seem to bend to the east.

Winds can be named for different reasons, but normally they are named for the direction *from* which they blow. The two bands of wind that lie between 30° north and 30° south of the equator are called the *trade winds.* (They are called this because sailors once relied on them for sailing their trading ships.) The wind bands north and south of the trade winds (between 30° and 60°) are called the *prevailing westerlies.* The wind bands blowing from the North and South Poles are called *polar easterlies.*

Color Code	
Polar Easterlies	Blue
Trade Winds	Red
Prevailing Westerlies	Yellow

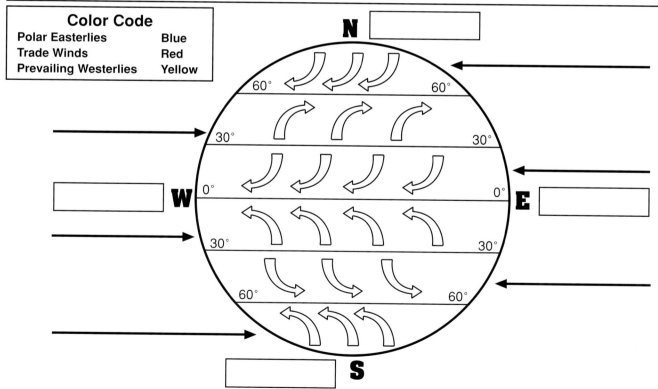

Bonus Box: Research the name of the effect that causes wind moving toward the equator to bend to the west and wind moving away from the equator to bend to the east. Write your answer on the back of this sheet.

Note to the teacher: Provide each student with crayons or colored pencils.

Clouds and Precipitation

Stir up a storm of student interest in clouds and precipitation using this collection of creative activities!

Background for the Teacher

- Clouds are masses of small water droplets or ice crystals floating in the air.
- There are three main cloud types. Latin names describe their characteristics: *stratus* (layered or spread out), *cumulus* (heap or pile), and *cirrus* (curly or hairlike). Other Latin terms used to describe clouds are *alto* (higher level) and *nimbus* (rain producing). The terms are combined to describe other cloud types: *stratocumulus, altostratus, nimbostratus, altocumulus, cumulonimbus, cirrostratus,* and *cirrocumulus.*
- Low clouds such as *stratus* and *stratocumulus* are usually less than 6,000 feet above sea level. Middle clouds such as *altostratus, altocumulus,* and *nimbostratus* usually form between 6,000 and 20,000 feet. High clouds such as *cirrus, cirrostratus,* and *cirrocumulus* may reach higher than 35,000 feet.
- Clouds form when water vapor cools and expands as it rises. The vapor *condenses* (changes from gas to liquid) onto dust particles and forms water droplets (or forms ice crystals in a process called *sublimation*).
- Evaporated water from oceans, lakes, rivers, plants, and moist soil contributes to cloud formation.
- Rain clouds are formed in three ways. *Convective clouds* are formed when the sun warms moist surface air, which rises and condenses into clouds. *Orographic clouds* form when warm, moist air lifts up over a mountain, where it cools and condenses. *Frontal clouds* are formed when masses of warm and cool air meet.
- *Fog* is a stratus cloud close to the earth's surface. Thin fog is called *mist* or *haze*.
- *Precipitation* comes in different forms—rain, snow, hail, sleet, and *graupel* (snow pellets)—depending on temperature and air conditions.

The puffy cloud in the dark sky floated like a marshmallow in hot chocolate.

The frightening black cloud was a roaring dragon spitting fire.

Creatively Cloudy
(Creative Writing, Critical Thinking)

Stimulate your students' imaginations and their creative-writing abilities with an outdoor cloud-watching activity. Tell students that for centuries people have imagined shapes like elephants, birds, and castles in clouds. This pastime is called *nephelococcygia* (nə fē lō kŏk ə jē ə). Spend a few minutes relaxing outside with your students on the next cloudy day. As they watch the clouds drift overhead, direct students to identify and describe the shapes they see. Upon returning to the classroom, have several student volunteers describe the cloud shapes they observed.

Next, explain to students that a *simile* is a comparison of two things using the words *like* or *as*. For example, "The puffy cloud in the dark sky floated *like* a marshmallow in hot chocolate." Further explain that a *metaphor* compares two things *without* using the words *like* or *as*. For example, "The frightening black cloud *was* a roaring dragon spitting fire." Next, have each student choose a cloud shape he observed and write a description of it using a simile or metaphor. Then direct the student to draw and cut out a cloud shape that matches his description. Have the student copy his description on his cloud cutout. Tape the clouds on the windows for everyone to enjoy.

Clearly Cool Cloud Books

Sector 7 by David Wiesner (Houghton Mifflin Company, 1999)

Snowflake Bentley by Jacqueline Briggs Martin (Houghton Mifflin Company, 1998)

Weather (Eyewitness Books series) by Brian Cosgrove (Alfred A. Knopf, Inc.; 1991)

Weather (Make It Work! series) by Andrew Haslam and Barbara Taylor (World Book, Inc.; 1997)

Weather Watch by Valerie Wyatt (Perseus Books, 1990)

Fog Magic
(Demonstration, Critical Thinking, Writing)

Clear up your students' questions about one type of fog formation with this simple demonstration. In advance, gather the following materials: two straight-sided clear glasses or jars (one 16 oz. and one 8 oz.), a sponge cut to fit the bottom of the larger jar, a piece of clear plastic wrap, an elastic band, boiling water, and ice water.

Begin the demonstration by explaining to students that *fog* is a cloud near the ground. If warm air is *saturated* (unable to hold any more moisture at its present temperature) and it moves across a cooler surface, the moisture condenses into fog. Next, place the sponge (representing the land) in the large jar and saturate it with ice water. Cover the jar with the plastic wrap, securing it with the elastic band. Fill half of the small jar with boiling water (representing the warm air) and carefully place it on top of the plastic wrap. Allow time for students to observe the results; then discuss them together as a class. *(Students should observe that the cool air in the large jar is warmed by the boiling water, leading to the formation of fog in it.)* If desired, culminate the activity by having each student recall a time when he observed a fog in a unique setting, such as on a summer morning near the ocean. Direct the student to write a descriptive paragraph explaining the unique conditions, including an explanation of how the fog formed. Encourage students to add illustrations to their paragraphs. Display students' work in an area titled "Fog Magic."

Cloud Collection
(Observation, Organizing Data, Art, Writing)

Help your students discover that weather events are related to certain cloud types with this unique cloud-observation activity. To begin the activity, guide students to complete "Cloudy Combinations" on page 15. Afterward, give each student a white, a gray, and a yellow crayon, along with an 8½" x 11" sheet of light blue paper. Direct the student to create a cloud collection chart like the one shown. Then, each day for one week, take your class outdoors to observe the clouds. Challenge each student to sketch the type of cloud she sees in the appropriate box on her chart. Upon returning to the classroom, have the student identify and label the cloud she drew, referring to her copy of "Cloudy Combinations" for help. Also have the student create a simple drawing to illustrate that day's weather, such as the sun, snowflakes, or raindrops. At the end of the week, involve students in making generalizations about the types of precipitation produced by various cloud types. To culminate the activity, direct each student to write a paragraph describing the clouds she observed and the precipitation associated with each cloud type. Your students will have practiced identifying cloud types and will have their very own reference for recent local cloud conditions.

Cloud Collection Chart

	Monday	Tuesday	Wednesday	Thursday	Friday
Cloud Illustration					
Cloud Type	Cumulus	Cumulonimbus	Cirrus	Cumulus	Altocumulus
Weather Illustration					
Weather Description	mostly sunny	hard rain	sunny	mostly sunny	light rain or drizzle

boiling water (warm air)

fog

cold, saturated sponge (cold earth)

11

Shifting Fronts
(Model, Critical Thinking)

Turn students into experts on fronts with this self-checking weather wheel. Discuss with students the definition of a *front* (a boundary between air masses of different temperatures). Then give each student an 11" x 17" copy of page 16, scissors, colored pencils or crayons, and a brad. Follow the directions below to guide each student in creating his wheel. After the wheels are created, demonstrate how to align the four circles to show the characteristics of each type of front and then discuss the resulting frontal information. Afterward, invite each student to use his wheel as he continues his study of weather fronts. Point out the self-checking key on the back of the wheel.

Directions:

1. Cut out the four wheel patterns. Then use the information at the bottom of the page to complete Steps 2–5.
2. At the top of each section on circle 1, write the term for each front and its matching letter. Then sketch the illustration for each front as shown in the diagram.
3. At the top of each section on circle 2, write the front description and its matching letter.
4. At the top of each section on circle 3, write the weather result and its matching letter.
5. At the top of each section on circle 4, write the meteorological symbol and its matching letter.
6. Color each wheel as desired.
7. Layer the circles one atop the other as shown. Connect the circles with a brad.
8. On the back of the wheel, copy each answer code behind its matching front.

My Life as a Water Droplet
(Creative Writing)

If a lacy snowflake, silvery raindrop, or icy hailstone could talk, it would tell you how rough it was growing up in a cloud! Explain to students how rain, snow, and hail form. (Rain forms when tiny droplets combine, making larger drops until they are too heavy to stay in the cloud. Snow forms when water droplets freeze onto ice crystals in a cloud. As these crystals fall, they collide and stick together to form snowflakes. Hail forms when ice crystals are tossed up and down in a cumulonimbus cloud and are coated with layers of freezing water). Next, challenge each student to imagine himself as one type of precipitation developing in a cloud. Instruct the student to combine scientific facts (such as the kind of cloud he was born in) with creative ideas (such as a description of his cloudy home or his feelings). After he edits his work, give the student a 9" x 12" sheet of construction paper. Have the student draw and cut out the precipitation's shape and write his story's final copy on the cutout. Then create a storm of stories by hanging each cutout with the student's work on a string from your classroom ceiling.

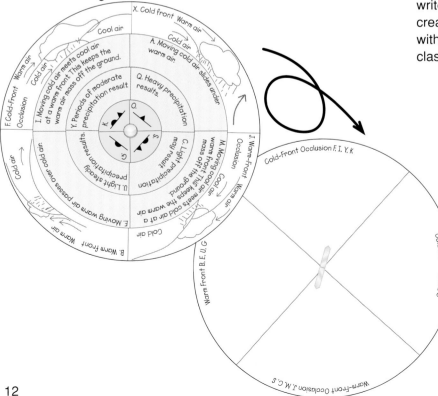

Hailbob's Bad Day
My name is Hailbob. This morning I was just a tiny ice crystal at the top of a puffy cumulonimbus cloud. The sun was shining and soon millions of other ice crystals and water droplets had crowded into my cloud. It began to get windy and everyone was pushing and shoving. I was thrown up and down and water droplets began to freeze to my skin. I was getting fatter and heavier by the minute. Suddenly I began to fall. I screamed for help but my friends were falling too! Down, down, down I dropped. Smash! Crackle! Ouch! I hit the window of a red truck.

Mountain "Mist-eries"
(Making a Model, Writing)

Why are mountaintops often covered with mist and clouds? Have students create models of these misty conditions to take the mystery out of this phenomenon. Begin by explaining to students that warm, moist air rising up a mountain's *windward* side (side facing the wind) cools quickly as it reaches higher altitudes. This cool moisture condenses into low clouds (mist or fog) and may produce rain or snow, depending on the altitude and air temperature. After the air has released most of its precipitation, the drier air moves down the *leeward* side (side away from the wind) of the mountain. Point out that this explains why the region on the windward side of a mountain range often gets more precipitation. For example, the annual precipitation on the windward (west) side of the Cascade Mountain Range in Washington averages over 135 inches; while on the leeward (east) side of this range, the average is six inches. Next, divide students into four groups, giving each group the materials listed below. Then guide each group through the steps to create its model.

Materials for each group of students:
small shoebox, blue and brown bulletin board paper, four cotton balls, glue, a supply of toothpicks, gray crayon, green paint, paintbrushes, scissors, salt dough (see the recipe shown), tape

Steps:
1. Cover the outside of the box with brown paper and the inside with blue paper.
2. Pull strands of cotton from one ball so they look like the wispy cirrus clouds that form high in the sky. Glue the strands to the blue paper at the top of the box.
3. Create a mountain landscape using the salt dough. Paint the landscape green.
4. Color the toothpicks gray to represent rain. Push them into the dough near the mountaintop on the windward side as shown.
5. Gently stretch and shape three cotton balls to look like puffy clouds. Glue each cloud onto the toothpicks.
6. Write a paragraph describing the formation of mountain mist. Tape your explanation to the top of the box.

> **Salt Dough Recipe**
>
> 8 c. flour
> 4 c. salt
> 4 c. water
> Knead the ingredients together until they are well blended.

Recipes for a Cloud
(Writing a Recipe)

Have students whip up recipes for clouds to heighten their understanding of cloud formation. Tell students that clouds form when moist air rises and becomes cooler. Use the background information on page 10 to explain the three ways rain clouds form: by *convection*, *lifting* (orographic), and *frontal activity*. Then divide the class into groups of three and give each group three file folder halves. On each file folder tab, have the group write a recipe title for a type of rain cloud formation. Then challenge the group to write a recipe for each type of formation, along with an illustrated example on each folder. After each group shares its recipes, collect the recipes and display them in a "recipe box" as shown. Have a student volunteer add decorative details to the box and label it "Cookin' Up Clouds."

Cookin' Up Clouds

Convective Cloud Recipe
Ingredients:
a measure of sunshine
a good dose of moist, cool air
some damp ground
a dash of warm air
Steps:
Let the sunshine warm the damp ground. Then have the warm air near the ground rise, carrying with it some of the ground's moisture. Finally, allow the warm air to cool as it rises so the moisture condenses. Yield: puffy, white, cumulus clouds.

The Truth About Snowflakes
(Literature, Math, Art)

Did your students know that they could search and search and never find two snowflakes that look alike? That's exactly what a man named Wilson Bentley spent his life doing! The picture book *Snowflake Bentley* by Jacqueline Briggs Martin, tells the true story of this man who turned his passion for nature and snow into a lifetime of photographing and studying the infinite variety of snowflakes. Read the book aloud to your students and discuss the story's message about the uniquely beautiful qualities of snowflakes. Afterward, distribute a copy of page 17, scissors, and an 8½" x 11" sheet of black construction paper to each student. Guide each student in creating her own unique snowflake. Then have each student glue her snowflake to the black paper to resemble a Wilson Bentley photograph. Allow time for each student to share her snowflake with the class, discussing its unique qualities. Display the snowflake creations on a bulletin board for everyone to study and enjoy.

Rainbow Bubble Show
(Experiment)

How do you make a rainbow? Here's a simple and fun demonstration using the magic of bubbles to show how rainbows form. Begin by asking students to list the physical qualities that bubbles and raindrops share, such as both are colorless and have rounded surfaces. Then have students hypothesize why rainbows are often observed during or after a rain shower. Explain to students that when light hits a raindrop's curved surface, it is reflected from different points along the drop's curve. This splits the light into the spectrum of colors that we call a rainbow.

Next, divide students into groups of three or four and designate an area near a window in which each group will work. Supply each group with the materials listed below. Appoint one student in each group to act as recorder, one to blow bubbles, and one to hold the construction paper background. Guide students through the steps below to complete the experiment; then discuss students' findings.

Materials for each group of 3–4 students:
shallow, clear dish of bubble soap; bubble-blowing wand; one 9" x 12" sheet of black construction paper; 1 sheet of notebook paper

Steps:
1. Direct each group to examine the bubble soap and describe its color. *(Students should observe that the bubble soap is clear and colorless.)*
2. Instruct the student holding the black construction paper to stand about two feet from the window, while remaining group members position themselves between the student and the window.
3. Have the designated student blow a few bubbles, catching one on the wand. Instruct her to move the wand slowly back and forth in front of the construction paper. Direct the group members to describe the colors they see and for the recorder to record the response.
4. Instruct the group to hypothesize why the colors appear in the bubbles despite the colorless nature of the soap. Have the recorder record the response. *(Guide students to understand that the light from the sun is reflected by the bubble. It is then split into a spectrum of colors by the bubble's curved shape.)*
5. If desired, repeat the experiment after adding a few drops of food coloring to the bubble soap. Have students blow a bubble and look for any differences in color. *(Students should observe that the bubble will not be affected by the food coloring.)* To prove that the food coloring is in the bubble, have each group pop a bubble onto white paper. *(Students should observe that the bubble leaves a food coloring stain on the paper.)*

Cloudy Combinations

Over 150 years ago, an English scientist named Luke Howard identified three basic types of clouds: *cumulus*, *stratus*, and *cirrus*. Howard added the terms *nimbus* to identify rain clouds and *alto* to describe higher clouds. Using a combination of these cloud types and terms, Howard identified several other types of clouds. Follow the directions below to learn more.

Directions: Read the information about the three basic clouds in the diagrams below. Then combine the Latin meanings to help you write the "definition" of each of the other types of clouds. Finally, sketch a picture of each cloud in the box.

Cumulus (Latin: "heap")

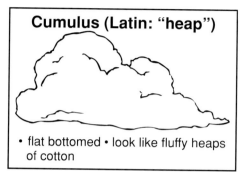

• flat bottomed • look like fluffy heaps of cotton

Stratus (Latin: "spread out")

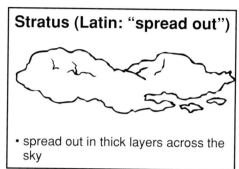

• spread out in thick layers across the sky

Cirrus (Latin: "curl")

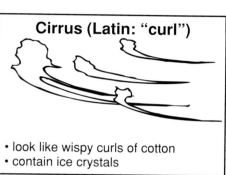

• look like wispy curls of cotton
• contain ice crystals

Cloud Name	Latin Meaning	Definition	Sketch
1. Cirrocumulus	_curl_ + _heap_	Cirrocumulus clouds are like puffy curls of cotton and hold ice crystals.	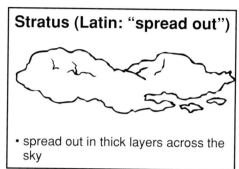
2. Cumulonimbus	_____ + _____		
3. Altocumulus	_____ + _____		
4. Nimbostratus	_____ + _____		
5. Cirrostratus	_____ + _____		
6. Altostratus	_____ + _____		
7. Stratocumulus	_____ + _____		

Note to the teacher: Use with "Cloud Collection" on page 11.

Patterns

Use with "Shifting Fronts" on page 12.

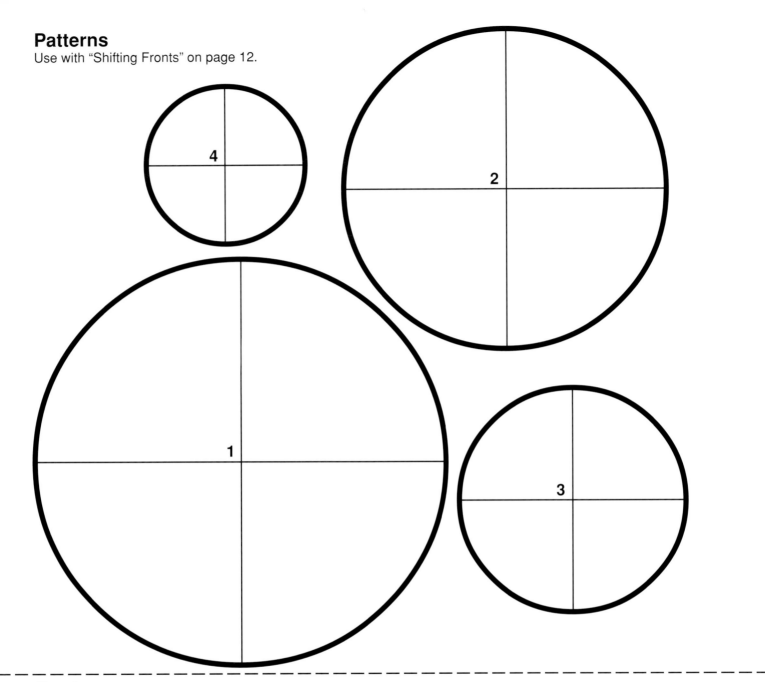

Fronts

X. Cold Front

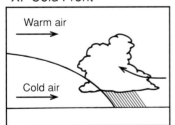
Warm air
Cold air

B. Warm Front

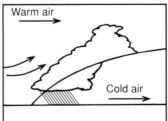
Warm air
Cold air

F. Cold-Front Occlusion

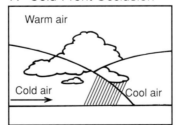
Warm air
Cold air   Cool air

J. Warm-Front Occlusion

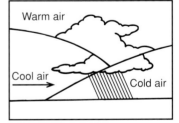
Warm air
Cool air   Cold air

Description of Front

A. Moving cold air slides under warm air.

E. Moving warm air passes over cold air.

I. Moving cold air meets cool air at a warm front. This keeps the warm air mass off the ground.

M. Moving cool air meets cold air at a warm front. This keeps the warm air mass off the ground.

Weather Result

Q. Heavy precipitation results.

U. Light, steady precipitation results.

Y. Periods of moderate precipitation result.

C. Light precipitation may result.

Symbols

O. ▲

G. ◖

K. ▲▲

S. ▲▲

Tantalizing, Tessellating Snowflakes

What does math have to do with snowflakes? Snow is formed when ice crystals collide and stick together. These snowflakes are *hexagons* (six-sided figures). Many geometric shapes, like hexagons, can *tessellate*, or fit together to make a pattern with no spaces or overlapping edges. Follow the directions below to create your own unique snowflake using the tessellating hexagon that has been drawn for you.

Directions:

1. Carefully cut out the tessellation along the bold cutting line. (Fig. 1)

Fig. 1

2. Fold the tessellation in half, being careful to line up the matching edges. (Fig. 2)

Fig. 2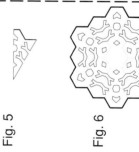

3. Carefully fold the tessellation in half again. (Fig. 3)

Fig. 3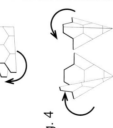

4. Fold the tessellation in thirds by first folding the left side to the center and then folding the right side over the left side. (Fig. 4)

Fig. 4

5. Snip designs into each side of the folded tessellation (being careful not to cut off a fold). (Fig. 5)

Fig. 5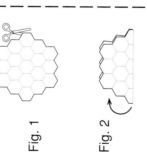

6. Unfold and admire your unique snowflake. (Fig. 6)

Fig. 6

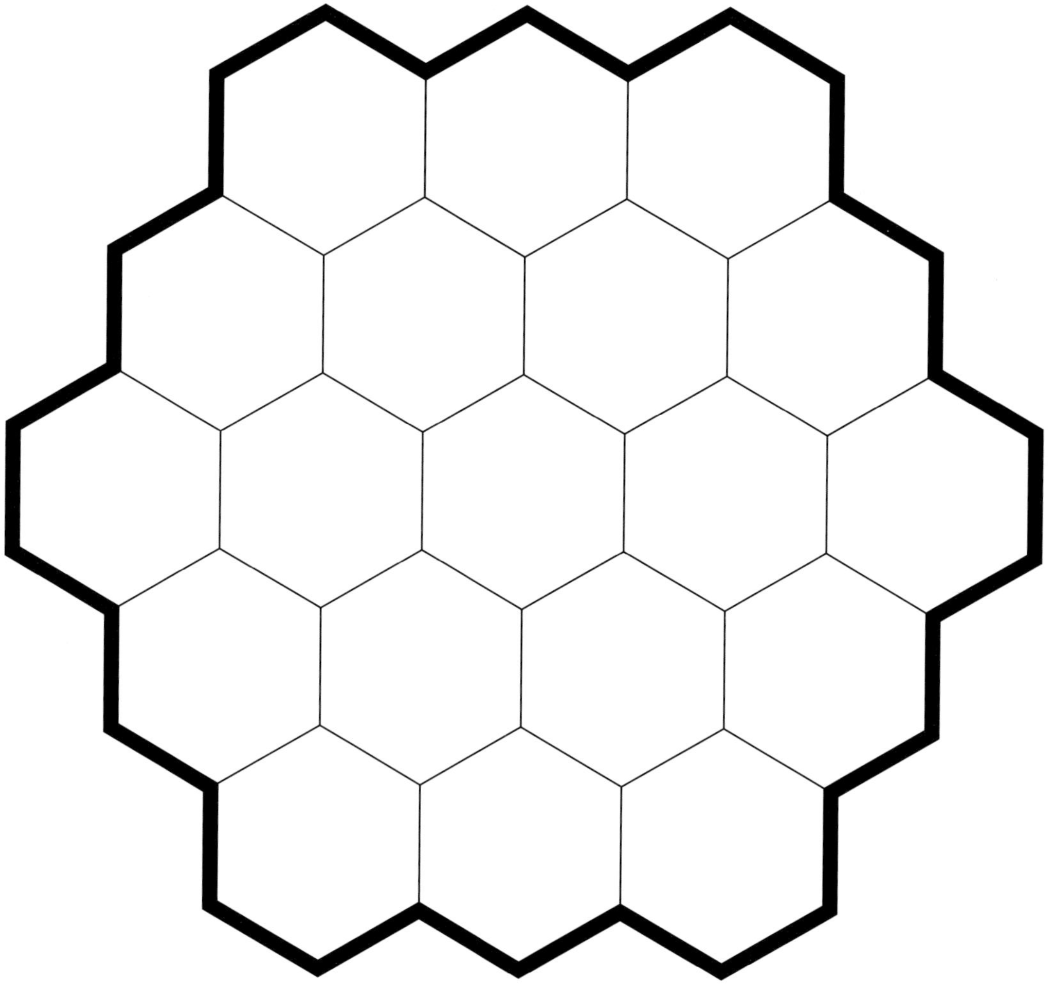

Note to the teacher: Use with "The Truth About Snowflakes" on page 14.

Storms

Immerse your students in this downpour of activities and reproducibles all about storms!

Blowin' in the Wind
(Concentration Game)

Your students will be blown away with this wind force game! Explain to students that wind speed is a major factor in the strength of a storm and that the *Beaufort Scale* is a tool used to categorize these speeds. On an overhead projector or sheet of chart paper, display a copy of the Beaufort Scale as shown on page 6, and then discuss it with students. Next, pair students and give each pair scissors and a copy of the game cards on page 24. Direct the pair to cut out the cards. To play the game, have each pair turn the cards facedown on a playing surface, scattering them so no two cards are overlapping. Instruct the first player to choose two cards. If she chooses an observation card and its matching Beaufort Scale card, she keeps the match and then draws two more cards. If her cards don't match, she puts them back, facedown, and then her partner takes a turn in the same manner. Play continues until all cards have been matched. The winner is the player with more cards at the end of the game. If desired, store game cards and a copy of the Beaufort Scale in a center for students to play in their spare time.

Background for the Teacher

- A storm is an *atmospheric cyclone,* or area of low pressure surrounded by winds that spiral inward. *Storms* consist of rain, freezing rain, snow, strong winds, or a combination of these.
- *Tornadoes,* also called *twisters* and *cyclones,* are spinning funnel clouds containing the most violent winds on Earth. Tornadoes spin counterclockwise in the Northern Hemisphere and clockwise in the Southern Hemisphere.
- A *waterspout* is a tornado that occurs over an ocean or a lake.
- *Hurricanes,* also called *typhoons* in the western Pacific Ocean and *cyclones* in the Indian Ocean, are storms with a diameter of 200 to 300 miles and wind speeds of 74 miles per hour or more. These winds rotate around the *eye,* or calm area in the center of the storm. *Wall clouds,* or storm clouds, surround the eye and produce the heaviest rain.
- A *tropical depression* is a storm with wind speeds of up to 31 miles per hour.
- A *tropical storm* has wind speeds of up to 73 miles per hour.
- *Blizzards* are blinding snowstorms with strong, cold winds blowing 35 miles per hour or more, temperatures as low as 10°F, and visibility of less than 500 feet.
- *Severe blizzards* have winds over 45 miles per hour, temperatures less than 10°F, and almost zero visibility.

Stormy Literature Selections

The Big Storm by Bruce Hiscock (Aladdin Paperbacks, 2000)

Lightning (Nature in Action series) by Stephen Kramer (Carolrhoda Books, Inc.; 1992)

The Magic School Bus Inside a Hurricane by Joanna Cole (Scholastic Inc., 1996)

The Storm by Marc Harshman (Cobblehill Books, 1995)

Storm (The Violent Earth series) by Jenny Wood (Thomson Learning, 1993)

Storm Warning: Tornadoes and Hurricanes (How's the Weather? series) by Jonathan D. Kahl (Lerner Publications Company, 1993)

Tornado (Nature in Action series) by Stephen Kramer (Carolrhoda Books, Inc.; 1992)

My, What Pressure!
(Making a Barometer)

How do meteorologists know when a storm is approaching? Many factors are taken into consideration, but understanding changes in air pressure helps predict when a storm will occur. Explain to students that when air pressure is high, the weather is often clear; when air pressure is low, the weather is often stormy. Next, help students make *barometers*—instruments used for measuring atmospheric pressure—to see if they can predict approaching stormy weather. Divide students into groups. Give each group the materials listed below and then guide them through the following steps. Have each student record her observations for one week (or longer if there hasn't been any rain in your area). Remind students of the relationship between high and low pressure and the weather.

Materials for each group: plastic or glass jar, strong rubber band, tape, piece of cardboard, drinking straw, marker, balloon, scissors, ruler, sheet of paper, or science journal

Steps:
1. Cut the balloon as shown and stretch the larger part across the mouth of the jar—but not too tightly.
2. Secure the balloon in place with a rubber band.
3. Cut the straw to make a pointed end as shown. Tape the opposite end of the straw to the balloon.
4. Have one group member hold the cardboard next to the jar. Make a mark and then draw a line across the cardboard where the straw now points.
5. Add three lines above and three lines below this first line, each one-fourth inch apart. Label the top three lines "high" and the bottom three lines "low."
6. Place your barometer on a shelf or table near a wall. Tape the cardboard piece to the wall so that the pointed end of the straw is aligned with the middle line.
7. Each day, record the date, whether the air pressure is high or low, and the outside weather conditions on a sheet of paper or in a science journal.
8. After one week, review your recordings. What conclusions can you make about high and low air pressure and the type of weather each signals? Explain.

Lightning Game
(Lightning Facts Game, Research)

Spark your students' interest in lightning with this Jeopardy®-like game. Divide students into five groups and give each group five 5" x 8" index cards. Assign each group one of the following lightning categories: *Types, Effects, How Lightning Occurs, Interesting Facts,* and *Safety.* Direct each group to research five facts about its category. Next, have each group use the facts to write a different question and corresponding answer on each card, and then label the other side of the cards with its category. Instruct each group to rank its cards in levels of difficulty ranging from $100 (easiest) to $500 (hardest) and write that number below the category label.

Set up the gameboard by writing the above categories across the top of a chalkboard. Collect the cards and tape them in numerical order under the correct categories. Next, divide students again so that one person from each of the original groups is now on a team. To start, have a player from one team choose a category and dollar amount. Read the answer on the chosen card aloud and have the student respond in question form. (Allow the student to confer with her teammates, if necessary.) If she answers correctly, award her team the dollar amount on the card and then have a different teammate choose the next category and dollar amount. If she answers incorrectly, give the next team a chance to answer. Play proceeds until all cards have been chosen. The winner is the team with the highest dollar amount. If desired, add a "lightning round" with challenging teacher-made cards and a 30-second time limit for answering.

Types
$500

Q: What is ball lightning?
A: It looks like a glowing, fiery ball and disappears after floating for several seconds.

Effects
$400

Q: What is about 60,000°F?
A: The temperature to which lightning can heat the air around it.

How Lightning Occurs
$300

Q: What is a thunderstorm?
A: During this storm, particles collide and become electrically charged.

Interesting Facts
$200

Q: Who is Benjamin Franklin?
A: This man proved that lightning is electricity.

Safety
$100

Q: What is a lightning rod?
A: This is made of metal and helps protect buildings from lightning.

Flash! Boom! Bang!
(Thunder Demonstration)

Your students will get a real bang out of this demonstration showing the relationship between thunder and lightning. Explain to students that *thunder* is the sound given off by the explosive expansion of air that has been heated by a lightning stroke, usually during a thunderstorm. Even though thunder and lightning occur simultaneously, the sound of thunder takes much longer than the sight of lightning to reach us. This is because light travels at approximately 186,000 miles per second and sound travels at approximately 1,100 feet (or one-fifth of a mile) per second.

To demonstrate this relationship, have one student, representing lightning, stand by the classroom light switch(es). Give a second student, representing thunder, an opened paper lunch bag and position him at the front of the classroom facing his classmates. Turn off the lights. Direct the demonstration as follows: Lightning flips the light switch(es) on and off once to represent a bolt of lightning. The rest of the students begin slowly counting seconds in this way: one thousand one, one thousand two, and so on. At the same time, Thunder blows inside the lunch bag and traps a giant breath of air. Then, holding the bag securely closed, he waits until the class reaches ten seconds, and then he hits the bottom of the air-filled bag, creating a sound similar to that of thunder.

Help students determine how far away this "lightning" is. Divide the total number of seconds counted *(ten)* by five (because sound travels one-fifth of a mile per second) to get the number of miles away the lightning struck *(2 miles)*. Practice this equation by giving students different time periods. For example, 100 seconds ÷ 5 = 20 miles away, 36 seconds ÷ 5 = 7.2 miles away, 13 seconds ÷ 5 = 2.6 miles away, etc.

A Storm Is Coming!
(Movement Game)

Create a thunderstorm right in your classroom with this thigh-patting, foot-stomping demonstration! Have students stand in a circle in an area of the classroom. Explain to students that most thunderstorms have three stages: *cumulus stage* (clouds gather), *mature stage* (heaviest rain), and *dissipating stage* (end of the storm). Begin your thunderstorm simulation by completing the first action. Then, starting with the student on your left, direct each successive student to copy the action until the whole circle repeats it. Begin the next action in the same fashion, having each student continue one action until it is her turn to begin the next one. Contine in the same manner until your "thunderstorm" has developed. Finally, repeat the actions in reverse order to show the storm dissipating. If desired, allow students to add to your storm by suggesting different movements to simulate additional types of weather, such as sleet or hail.

Action/Weather
raise hands from chest to up over head in an arc/**clouds**

gentle thigh patting/**light rain**

medium thigh patting/**rain**

hard thigh patting and wind noises with your mouth/ **rain and wind**

stomping and wind noises/**heavy rain and wind**

stomping, wind noises, and loud clapping/**heavy rain, wind, and thunder**

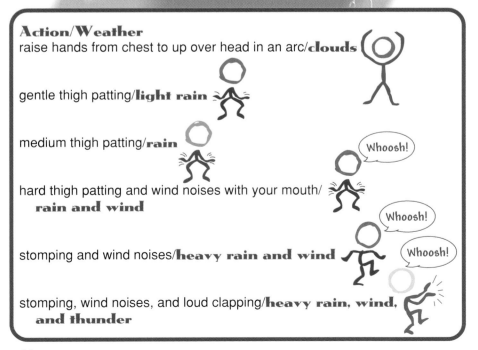

Takin' a Tornado Trek
(Mapping Activity, Explanatory Writing)

Sweep students off their feet with this activity telling about the largest tornado in American history—the 1925 Tri-State Tornado. Explain to students that most tornadoes last less than an hour, traveling a distance of about 20 miles at a speed of 10–25 miles per hour. Some tornadoes can even last several hours, traveling 200 miles or more at speeds of up to 60 miles per hour. Then share with students the following facts about the devastating Tri-State Tornado: it had the third fastest traveling speed, it exerted continuous force resulting in damage throughout most of its life span, and it lasted a record 3.5 hours! Further explain that in 1925 there were no National Weather Service warnings, radars, or satellites to give people any advance warning about the tornado.

Next, make a transparency of a blank United States map. Then use the information on the diagram at the right to help students track this infamous tornado's progress through Missouri, Illinois, and Indiana. Discuss the different aspects of the tornado, such as the amount of time it took to get from town to town and the number of miles it covered. If desired, follow up by discussing with students how the effects of such a storm might be different today because of technological advancements.

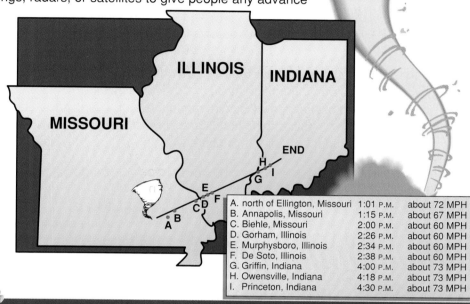

A. north of Ellington, Missouri	1:01 P.M.	about 72 MPH
B. Annapolis, Missouri	1:15 P.M.	about 67 MPH
C. Biehle, Missouri	2:00 P.M.	about 60 MPH
D. Gorham, Illinois	2:26 P.M.	about 60 MPH
E. Murphysboro, Illinois	2:34 P.M.	about 60 MPH
F. De Soto, Illinois	2:38 P.M.	about 60 MPH
G. Griffin, Indiana	4:00 P.M.	about 73 MPH
H. Owensville, Indiana	4:18 P.M.	about 73 MPH
I. Princeton, Indiana	4:30 P.M.	about 73 MPH

A Gem of a Storm
(Classifying Information)

Help students polish up their knowledge of blizzards with this classifying activity. Write the Blizzard Facts listed below on a chalkboard or sheet of chart paper. Next, give each student one sheet of white drawing paper and a black marker or crayon. Guide students through the following steps to create a gem of a study guide!

corner

Blizzard Facts
- wear a bright-colored coat, layered clothing, boots, gloves, and a hat
- solid white ground
- central and eastern Canada
- wind speeds 35 MPH or greater
- never go out in a storm alone
- if stuck outside, keep moving and don't fall asleep
- temperatures 10°F or less
- northern Great Plains of the United States
- air white with blowing snow
- heavy, cold air forces warm, moist air to rise
- if a storm watch or warning is issued, stay inside
- some areas of Russia
- white or gray sky
- visibility 500 feet or less

Steps:
1. Fold the paper in half; then fold it in half again.
2. Turn down the corner at the fold about 1¹/₂ inches as shown.
3. Unfold the paper. (Students should have four sections with a diamond shape in the middle as shown.) Use a marker or crayon to outline the center diamond and each resulting section.
4. Write Blizzard in the diamond shape. Then write one of the following titles in each of the other sections: Conditions, Features, Locations, and Safety.
5. Read each of the posted Blizzard Facts. Think about each fact, writing each one in the appropriate section.

21

Do the Hurricane Spin
(Hurricane Simulation, Drawing a Diagram)

Put a little movement into your study of hurricanes with these two fun outdoor activities. Take students outside to an open, flat area, such as a ball field, and complete each activity below. Once back inside the classroom, explain to students that a hurricane has four parts in which the wind speeds are significantly different: (1) the *eye* (calm), (2) the *eye wall* or *inner hurricane* (about 120–150 MPH), (3) the *middle hurricane* (about 74 MPH), and (4) the *outer hurricane* (about 40 MPH). Then give each student a sheet of white paper. Direct the student to draw a diagram of a hurricane and then label the four areas with the information above.

Activity 1

Pair students. Explain that with this activity, each student will feel a force pushing him outward from his partner. Further explain that the force pushing him out is the same type of force that pushes the winds out from the eye of a hurricane—leaving the eye calm. Then direct each pair to hold hands and carefully spin around two or three times as shown. Ask student volunteers to share what they felt as they spun around.

Eye

Activity 2

Divide students into groups of five or six. Have each group form a line, standing an arm's length apart. Instruct each student to place her hands on the shoulders of the students next to her as shown. Designate the student at one end of the line to represent the eye. Direct the rest of the line to begin walking around in a circle so that the Eye moves very little. Stop students and explain that in a hurricane the winds spin around the eye, but the eye stays very still in comparison. If desired, allow them to repeat the activity several times, moving at different speeds and taking turns being the Eye.

Tornado

Tornados are so powerful they can blow off a roof top.

Bulletin Board Bonanza
(Research, Art Activity)

Challenge students to create a blizzard of facts, a gust of gale-force winds, a whirlwind of information, and a downpour of details with this unique bulletin board activity. In advance, divide a bulletin board into four equal sections. Then divide students into four groups. Give each group an assortment of supplies, such as scissors, glue, construction paper, markers, glitter, string, etc. Then assign each group one of the bulletin board sections and a storm—a blizzard, hurricane, tornado, or thunderstorm. Direct each group to brainstorm facts it has learned about its assigned storm and then use the provided materials to decorate its section as desired (see example shown). Instruct each group to be creative and to use as many facts as possible. Award small prizes for the most original art and the most fact-filled sections.

A Storm Is Approaching
(Role-Playing)

Put your students on "storm alert" with this role-playing activity. Divide students into groups of four. Have each group choose a weather emergency, such as a tornado, hurricane, blizzard, or severe thunderstorm. Next, have each group member choose one of the created jobs from the box below. Have each group work together to research its assigned storm to find information relating to each job. For example, a meteorologist would need to know the weather signs showing approaching severe weather. Next, direct each group to prepare a weather broadcast, giving the public the facts it needs to prepare for the approaching storm. Allow each group enough time to practice its lines and gather props. Then have each group "broadcast" its report to the class.

> **Meteorologist**—relates the details of the approaching storm to the public
> **Community Safety Manager**—gives information on what the community can do to ensure public safety during this storm
> **Family Safety Manager**—gives information on what individual families can do to ensure safety at home during this storm
> **Reporter**—interviews the safety managers

A Storm of Poetry
(Writing Poetry, Art)

Storm into a great poetry lesson! Begin by asking students if they have ever noticed how some words create a visual image when said out loud. For example, ask students what comes to mind when they hear the words *dash, blustering, brewing,* and *snugly.* Next, remind students that poetry is a form of writing that uses words to evoke images in a reader's mind. Describe the form of poetry called *tanka.* Tanka is an Asian form of verse often about nature and made up of five unrhymed lines with a specific number of syllables. On a chalkboard or an overhead transparency, copy the poem shown. Share the poem with students, identifying the number of syllables in each line.

Direct each student to write his own tanka poem about one type of storm he has been studying. Then give each student a sheet of construction paper, markers, and scissors. Instruct the student to make a cutout in the shape of his chosen storm. Have the student copy his poem onto the cutout and illustrate it with details from his poem as shown. Display students' finished products on a bulletin board titled "A Storm of Poetry."

A storm is brewing! (5)

With blustering winds and snow. (7)

A blizzard perhaps? (5)

We better dash home quickly. (7)

We'll be snugly warm inside! (7)

Game Cards

Beaufort Scale 8	Beaufort Scale 3		That small maple tree is swaying gently.
Beaufort Scale 2	Beaufort Scale 11	Evacuate immediately! The winds are over 80 MPH!	The storm's winds are up to 69 MPH and are causing a lot of damage!
Beaufort Scale 5	Beaufort Scale 10	You may need a stronger umbrella; the winds are 29 MPH!	It's so calm. It feels like there is no wind at all.
Beaufort Scale 12–17	Beaufort Scale 7	The leaves in that yard are being blown around.	Some of the twigs are breaking off of that tree.
Beaufort Scale 0	Beaufort Scale 9	That house just lost three shingles from its roof!	That whole tree is moving in the 34-MPH wind.
Beaufort Scale 6	Beaufort Scale 1	The light breeze feels nice and cool.	The smoke from that chimney is slowly blowing toward the north.
		That tree just pulled right out of the ground!	

24

Note to the teacher: Use with "Blowin' in the Wind" on page 18.

Name _____

Tracking Hurricane Windy

Track Hurricane Windy as it moves north through the Caribbean. Use the grid lines *(latitude and longitude* lines) on the map to chart Windy's progress. Make a hurricane symbol—@—to show the hurricane's location at each point. Then answer the questions that follow. Use the back of this page if you need more space.

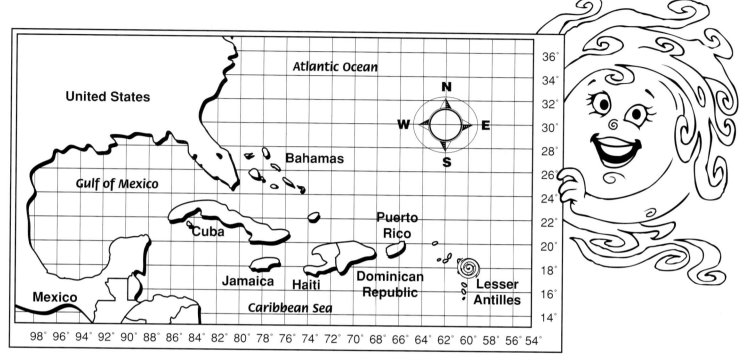

Clues:

1. Hurricane Windy is spotted off of the Lesser Antilles. (18°N, 60°W)
2. The *trade winds,* or large wind belts north of the equator, push Windy to the northwest. (21°N, 63°W)
3. Windy continues to move in a westerly direction. (21°N, 67°W)
4. Windy passes near the Dominican Republic and Haiti. (22°N, 70°W)
5. Winds push Windy northwest. (23°N, 75°W)
6. Passing through the Bahamas, Windy heads for Florida. (25°N, 78°W)
7. As Windy approaches the mainland, it continues north and travels along the coast. (28°N, 78°W)
8. Windy moves toward the coasts of Georgia and South Carolina. (31°N, 80°W)
9. The *prevailing westerlies,* strong winds blowing around the earth from west to east, push Windy back out to sea! (33°N, 77°W)
10. North Carolina gets heavy rains, but Windy continues in an northeasterly fashion. (36°N, 75°W)

Questions:

1. Which islands were directly hit by Windy? _____
2. Which island do you think got heavier rains from Windy: Puerto Rico or the Dominican Republic? Why? _____
3. What caused Windy to turn east, back out to sea? _____
4. Do you think the people in Florida should have been evacuated when Windy passed through the Bahamas? Why or why not? _____

©2000 The Education Center, Inc. • *Investigating Science • Weather & Climate* • TEC1732 • Key p. 48

Note to the teacher: Use this page independently, as a follow-up to "Do the Hurricane Spin" on page 22, or to track a real hurricane.

Twistin' in the USA

Tornadoes can occur just about anywhere in the world. Most tornadoes in the United States occur in an area called *Tornado Alley*.

Directions:

1. Choose one color for each range of numbers in the key using a different-colored pencil or crayon.
2. Use the key and the table below to color the map according to the average number of tornadoes occurring in each state each year.
3. Answer the map questions at the bottom of the page.

Average Number of Tornadoes per Year

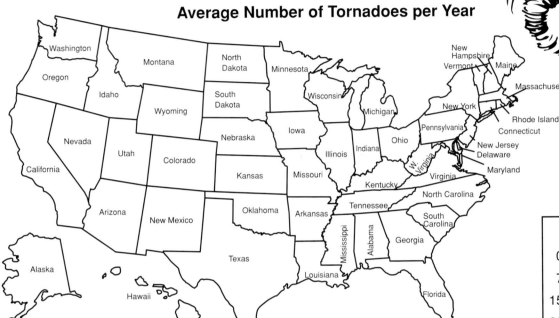

Key

0–7.4	color
7.5–15	color
15.1–22.6	color
22.7 and above	color

Average Number of Tornadoes Annually

State	Avg	State	Avg
Alabama	19	Montana	3.5
Alaska	0	Nebraska	34
Arizona	3.8	Nevada	0.6
Arkansas	18.4	New Hampshire	2.5
California	2.9	New Jersey	1.6
Colorado	14.2	New Mexico	8.5
Connecticut	1.7	New York	3.4
Delaware	0.85	North Carolina	10.3
Florida	36.3	North Dakota	14.6
Georgia	21.1	Ohio	13
Hawaii	0.62	Oklahoma	55.3
Idaho	1.3	Oregon	0.9
Illinois	28	Pennsylvania	6.6
Indiana	22.9	Rhode Island	0.04
Iowa	25.5	South Carolina	8.9
Kansas	46.6	South Dakota	22.6
Kentucky	7.8	Tennessee	11
Louisiana	18.8	Texas	124.2
Maine	2.8	Utah	1.36
Maryland	2.3	Vermont	1
Massachusetts	4.5	Virginia	5.24
Michigan	14.7	Washington	1
Minnesota	17.3	West Virginia	1.9
Mississippi	21.8	Wisconsin	17.3
Missouri	29.5	Wyoming	6.7

Questions:

1. What states do you think are included in Tornado Alley? Why? _____

2. Which state has a high number of tornadoes each year, but is not part of Tornado Alley? _____

3. Think about the geography of the states in Tornado Alley. Are they mountainous, plains, or coastal? Do you think the type of geography has anything to do with the number of tornadoes a state gets? Why or why not? _____ _____

And the Record Goes To...

Directions: Use the record-breaking facts below to answer the questions that follow.

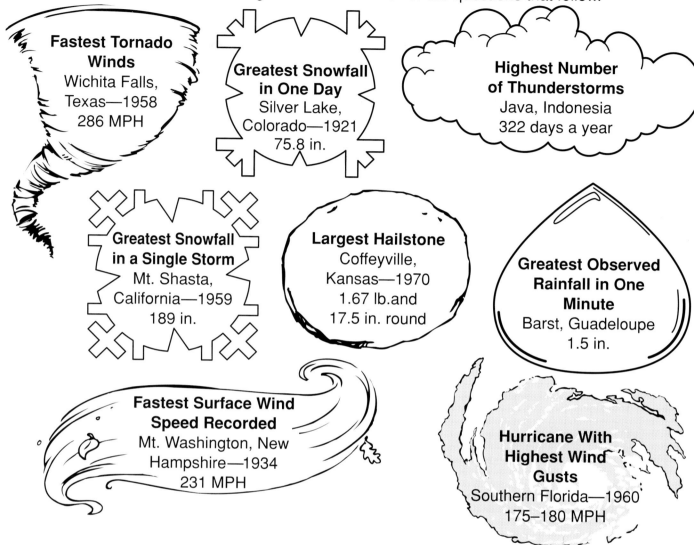

1. What is the difference in the amount of snowfall Mt. Shasta had during a single storm and Silver Lake had during a single day? _____

2. For about how many days out of each year are there no thunderstorms in Java? _____

3. If the rain in Barst continued to pour for one hour at the same rate, how many inches of rain would Barst have gotten? _____

4. Which had the highest (fastest) winds: the hurricane in Florida or the tornado in Texas? By how much? _____

5. Given the information in the facts above, which record is the most recent? How long ago did it occur? _____

6. The minimum wind speed of a hurricane is 74 MPH. How much greater were the wind gusts in the South Florida hurricane? _____

Bonus Box: On another sheet of paper, design an award to give to one of the above record breakers.

Note to the teacher: Facts current as of 1992.

Predicting the Weather

Turn your students into amateur weather watchers with this bright forecast of sunny ideas, experiments, and reproducibles!

Background for the Teacher

- The World Meteorological Organization (WMO) is an international organization whose members exchange weather information and forecasts.
- Weather data is sent to the WMO from land-based observation stations, radar systems, weather balloons, airplanes, ships, and satellites.
- *Meteorologists,* scientists who study and forecast the weather, use data from measurements taken throughout the day to predict the development and movement of future weather systems.
- Meteorologists use weather maps and mathematical computer models to help them make both short-range and extended (long-range) forecasts.
- Various weather instruments monitor the atmosphere. An *electronic thermometer* registers the highest and lowest temperatures of the day. A *hygrometer* shows the amount of water vapor in the air. A *barometer* measures the air pressure. A *weather vane* shows the direction of the wind. An *anemometer* checks wind speed. A *rain gauge* measures rainfall or snowfall.
- The National Weather Service of the United States and the Atmospheric Environment Service of Canada use radio and television broadcasts, newspapers, and the Internet to provide weather forecasts, watches, warnings, and advisories to the public.

Meteorology Mobile
(Research, Making a Mobile)

"Mobile-ize" students' thinking about meteorology with this cooperative project. Explain to students that *meteorology* is the science of measuring, studying, and predicting the weather. Next, divide students into groups of four. Give each group a clothes hanger, 12 large index cards, markers, scissors, a hole puncher, and yarn. Direct each group to label its cards as shown, using 11 of the cards to spell *meteorology* in colorful letters. Have each group write a title and its members' names on the 12th card. With the help of reference materials, have each group write on the back of each letter card an appropriate sentence related to meteorology that starts with the letter on its front. (For example, letter *M:* Many different kinds of instruments are used to predict the weather; letter *R:* Radar is used to locate and track clouds and storms.) Then have each group attach the cards to the clothes hanger and hang it in a prominent place.

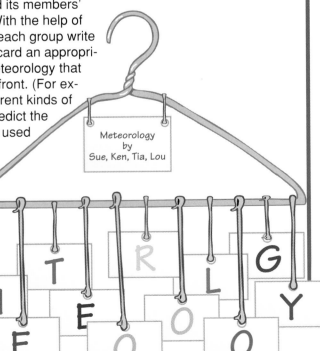

Meteorology
by
Sue, Ken, Tia, Lou

Weather Watchers' Literature List

It's Raining Cats and Dogs: All Kinds of Weather and Why We Have It by Franklyn Mansfield Branley (Houghton Mifflin Company, 1987)

Weather (Eyewitness Books series) by Brian Cosgrove (Alfred A. Knopf, Inc.; 1991)

The Weather Companion: An Album of Meteorological History, Science, and Folklore by Gary Lockhart (John Wiley & Sons, Inc.; 1988)

Weather Explained: A Beginner's Guide to the Elements (Your World Explained series) by Derek M. Elsom (Henry Holt & Company, Inc.; 1997)

Weather Forecasting by Gail Gibbons (Aladdin Paperbacks, 1993)

Weather Watch: Forecasting the Weather (How's the Weather? series) by Jonathan D. W. Kahl (Lerner Publications Company, 1996)

Folklore Forecasts
(Conducting a Survey, Graphing)

Does a groundhog *really* know if winter is ending? Do a grasshopper's chirrups *really* mean the temperature is rising? Have students examine familiar weather sayings to prepare for an investigative graphing activity. Give each student a copy of page 34. Together, discuss the meaning of each saying. Have students add additional sayings common to your region to the back of the page. Next, have the class select any six sayings on page 34 and mark each one with an asterisk. For homework, have each child poll ten relatives and friends, tallying their responses about whether or not they believe these six sayings are true. When the polling has been completed, help students combine the data collected into a double bar graph for a bulletin board titled "Folklore Forecasts: Fact or Fiction?" (see the example shown). If desired, follow up the activity by challenging interested students to find any scientific evidence that can authenticate one or more sayings; then have them report their findings to the class.

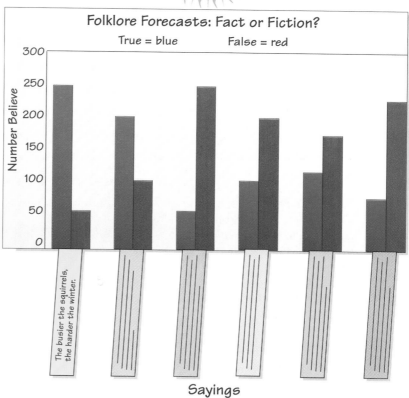

Folklore Forecasts: Fact or Fiction?
True = blue   False = red

Look Who's on the Six O'Clock News!
(Reading a Weather Map, Making a Presentation)

Will it be a "pleezy" day, or will it "fozzle"? Let your students make predictions such as these as they become television meteorologists for a day. In advance, collect weather maps from local newspapers, one map for each pair of students plus one extra. Make a transparency of the extra map; then mount each remaining map on a different sheet of construction paper. Use the transparency to teach students how to interpret a weather map's symbols. Point out the map's key, explaining that precipitation symbols may vary slightly from map to map. Next, have students recall and discuss what television meteorologists do during broadcasts, such as provide current weather conditions, make forecasts, etc. Then pair students. Give each pair a weather map on which to base a weather presentation similar to one done by a television meteorologist. Have one partner be responsible for explaining the weather conditions indicated on the pair's assigned map and the other predict the next day's weather based on those conditions. Challenge each presenter to invent words that can describe the current or predicted outdoor conditions. For example, "fozzle" is a mixture of fog and drizzle, "pleezy" is a day that is pleasant but breezy, and "snirt" is a concoction of snow and dirt. Perhaps you'll discover a future forecaster among your presenters! For more practice, follow up with the reproducible weather-map activity on page 35.

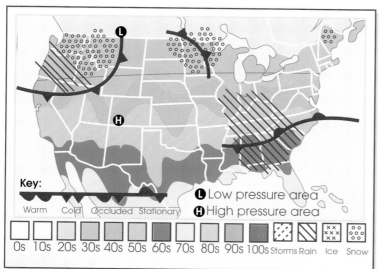

Key:
Warm   Cold   Occluded   Stationary
L Low pressure area
H High pressure area

0s 10s 20s 30s 40s 50s 60s 70s 80s 90s 100s Storms Rain Ice Snow

Weather-Probing Tools
(Research, Art)

What kind of instruments are used in weather forecasting? How do they work? How do they make weather forecasting easier? Challenge students to discover the answers to these questions by researching these valuable tools. Divide students into ten groups. Assign each group a different weather instrument from the list below. Have group members use encyclopedias, informational books, and the Internet to summarize the role their assigned weather instrument plays in making forecasts. Have the group attach its summary to a poster that includes a picture of the instrument and one or more scenes showing where or how the instrument could be used. If desired, offer extra credit to groups that make models of the instruments and demonstrate their use. Then display the posters and models in your school library to inspire younger students to become weather watchers.

Weather Instruments
- thermometer
- barometer
- weather vane
- anemometer
- hygrometer
- rain gauge
- radar
- weather balloon
- weather satellite
- ocean buoy

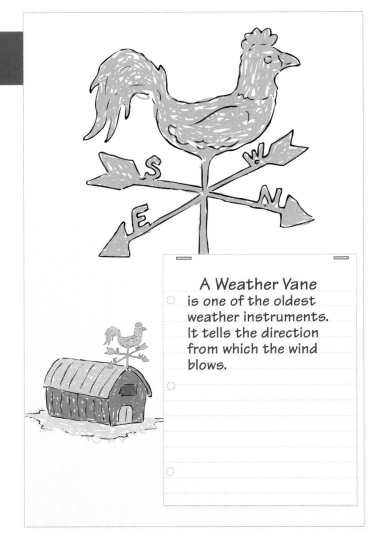

A Weather Vane is one of the oldest weather instruments. It tells the direction from which the wind blows.

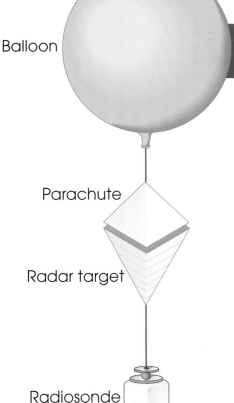

Balloon

Parachute

Radar target

Radiosonde

Weather-Balloon Wizardry
(Writing)

Let the blending of scientific facts and a little bit of fiction send your students up, up, and away with weather balloons! Explain to students that meteorologists regularly send weather balloons into the atmosphere. Also explain that each balloon has a special weather instrument—a *radiosonde*—attached to it that includes a radio transmitter that sends data back to a weather station. The radiosonde measures temperature *(the degree of heat in the atmosphere)*, air pressure *(the weight of the air pressing down on the earth)*, and humidity *(the amount of water or water vapor in the air)*. Point out that the balloon bursts at an altitude of about 19 miles and that a parachute carries the instrument safely back to the earth's surface.

Next, assign each student a different U.S. city. Direct him to go online at **www.wxusa.com** or a similar Web site to gather weather information about his assigned city. Then challenge him to write an imaginary story about a wee weather wizard named Willard whose job is to go up on the next balloon, gather weather data to make a local forecast for his city, and then parachute back to the earth. After students share their stories, tape the tales to the strings of inflated balloons and display them on a bulletin board titled "The High-Flyin' Tales of Weather Wizard Willard."

The Long and Short of Weather Forecasting
(Making Judgments)

Help students keep their weather eyes open by having them judge the accuracy of both short-range and long-range forecasts for one week. On Monday, copy on chart paper the long-range forecast from the Sunday paper. Explain to students that a typical long-range forecast is for five days. Then record Sunday's short-range forecast (also from Sunday's paper) below its long-range forecast. Explain that this type of forecast predicts the weather for periods of 18 to 36 hours. Point out to students that the long-range and short-range forecasts are the same on Sunday because they were predicted on the same day. Ask the class to recall Sunday's weather and determine the accuracy of the forecasts. Record the decisions by writing either "Right On," "Partially Correct," or "No Way" on the chart under each one. (See the example shown.)

Next, on Tuesday, record the previous day's short-range forecast (from Monday's paper). Have students compare this forecast to the long-range forecast and determine the accuracy of each one. Record the decisions on the chart. Repeat this process each morning during the week. At the end of the week, have each student write a paragraph comparing the accuracy of short-range and long-range forecasts; then discuss their responses.

Long-Range Forecast

SUN	MON	TUE	WED	THU
45	50	39	34	32
26	33	35	22	20
Right On	Partially Correct			

Short-Range Forecast

45	50
26	33
Right On	Right On

Hazardous Weather Announcements

Type	Issued	Example(s)
warning	when dangerous weather is expected or about to happen	severe thunderstorms, tornadoes, floods, flash floods, hurricanes, blizzards, ice storms, freezing temperatures, frost, high winds
watch	when current weather conditions could develop into a dangerous event for people and/or property	severe thunderstorms, tornadoes, floods, hurricanes, blizzards, ice storms
advisory	when an expected weather event is not serious enough for a watch or warning	snow, sleet, freezing rain, low wind chill, high heat index, high winds, dense fog

warning	watch	advisory

Warning! Hazardous Weather!
(Critical Thinking)

Turn young weather watchers into decision makers with this game about severe-weather announcements. In advance, copy the chart at the left onto poster board. Also make two copies of page 36. Keep one copy as an answer key; cut the other copy into strips. Use the poster to discuss with students the different types of announcements the National Weather Service issues. Next, divide students into six teams. Give each team four of the cut paper strips and three index cards. Direct the team to label each card with the name of a different kind of weather announcement as shown. Have Team 1 read to Team 2 the descriptor (not the type of announcement) from one of its strips. Ask Team 2 to confer and then hold up a card that tells the type of announcement it thinks that descriptor needs. Have Team 1 check its strip to confirm Team 2's answer. Use the answer key to double-check. If correct, give Team 2 one point. Continue play by having Team 2 read one of its descriptors to Team 3 and so on until all the descriptors have been read. Declare the team with the most points the winner.

Check Out Those Clouds!
(Word Analysis, Game)

Use this sky-watching game to help students understand that clouds can provide reliable clues about forecasting weather. First, write the names of the following clouds on the board: *stratus, stratocumulus, nimbostratus, altostratus, altocumulus, cirrostratus, cirrocumulus, cumulonimbus.* Next to them, write the following Latin words and their meanings: *alto* ("high"), *cirro* ("curl"), *cumulo* ("pile"), *nimbus* ("rain"), *stratus* ("layered"). Using the Latin words, help students decode the definition of each cloud name. Point out that three cloud types are associated with precipitation: *stratus* clouds with light rain, snow, or drizzle; *nimbostratus* clouds with steady snow or rain; and *cumulonimbus* clouds with heavy rain accompanied by thunder, lightning, sometimes hail, and, on rare occasions, a tornado. Explain to students that they will use the cloud names to play a game that helps them learn what kind of weather each type of cloud can bring. Divide students into groups of four, and give each group the materials listed below. Then guide each group through the steps below to make a gameboard and spinner for playing the game.

Materials: 12" x 18" sheet of blue construction paper; scissors; glue; 3 crayons: 1 yellow, 1 white, 1 black; 4 game markers; a die; a paper clip; a pencil; a ruler; a copy of the pattern on page 37

To make the gameboard:
1. Fold and cut the blue paper in half lengthwise.
2. Glue the strips together lengthwise—end to end—to make a 6" x 35" strip.
3. Place the paper strip in a vertical position. Cut out the spinner on the bold lines and glue it to the bottom of the paper strip as shown.
4. Use a yellow crayon to draw a sun in the strip's upper right-hand corner. Use a black crayon to label the sun "Finish."
5. Use a white crayon to draw a winding trail of 24 puffy clouds, stretching from the spinner to the sun. Then use a black crayon to label the cloud closest to the spinner "Start."

To play:
1. With her marker on Start, Player 1 rolls the die and moves her game marker toward the sun that number of clouds. Next, holding the paper clip and pencil on the spinner as shown, Player 1 spins and uses the words on the pattern to describe the cloud spun. Then the player follows the rules on the pattern to complete her turn. For example, if Player 1 spins "stratocumulus," she would describe it as a "layered pile" and not move her marker.
2. Players 2, 3, and 4 take their turns, following the directions in Step 1.
3. Play continues in this manner with each player, in turn, rolling the die, moving forward, spinning the spinner, and moving as directed during a round. The first player on each team to reach the sun is the winner.
4. Play additional rounds as time permits.

Thank You, Meteorologists!
(Brainstorming)

Use this brainstorming activity to help students understand how valuable weather forecasting can be when making everyday plans. Ask students to name different activities that weather forecasting enables them to plan. Expect responses such as deciding what clothes to wear and whether to play outdoors. List the activities on the board. Next, guide students' thinking to more important issues, such as a forecast that would make an airplane pilot redirect his course to avoid landing in strong winds or one that would force a building contractor to delay the pouring of concrete because falling rain could ruin it before it hardened. Then divide students into groups of four. Challenge each group to extend the list on the board, trying to add as many additional examples as possible in ten minutes. When time is up, have each group share its list with the class. Do you sense a newfound respect for weather forecasting in the air?

Weather-Symbol Characters
(Art, Writing)

Strengthen students' skills in interpreting weather symbols with this creative art and writing activity. Give each child a sheet of art paper, colored pencils, and an enlarged copy of the weather-symbol chart below. Direct the student to use as many of the chart's weather symbols as possible to create a humanlike character named Weather Symbol Sam (or Sally). Have the student also record in the lower right-hand corner of the paper the number of *different* symbols he used in his drawing.

When the drawings are finished, have each student trade his creation with a classmate. Challenge each child to find the weather symbols in his classmate's picture, outline them with a black marker, and list them on the back of the paper (have him refer to the number recorded in the corner to see how many he should find). Then have him write an adventure story in which that character (Sam or Sally) experiences at least three of the weather conditions he listed on the back of the paper. When the stories have been finished, have the authors give the pictures and stories to the original artists to share with the class. Then display the drawings and their accompanying stories on a bulletin board titled "Weathering the Weather with Sam and Sally."

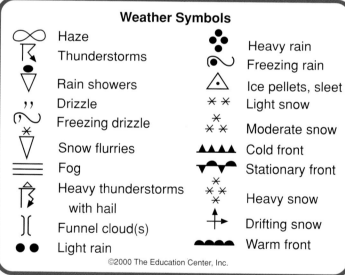

Weather Symbols

∞	Haze		
	Thunderstorms	⣿	Heavy rain
	Rain showers		Freezing rain
	Drizzle	△	Ice pellets, sleet
	Freezing drizzle	* *	Light snow
	Snow flurries	* *	Moderate snow
≡	Fog	▲▲▲▲	Cold front
	Heavy thunderstorms with hail	▼▼▼	Stationary front
	Funnel cloud(s)	* *	Heavy snow
••	Light rain		Drifting snow
			Warm front

©2000 The Education Center, Inc.

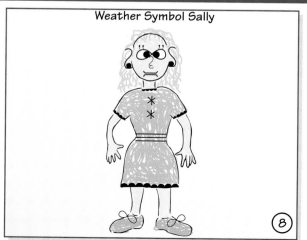

Weather Symbol Sally

Who's Who in Weather Forecasting?
(Research)

Help students appreciate the historical development of weather forecasting by having them take a closer look at the contributions or achievements of important scientists. Pair students. Assign each pair a different name from the list below. Direct each pair to research its scientist and write the following information on the shape of a stepping stone cut from gray construction paper: the scientist's name, the year the contribution was made, and a sentence or two summarizing the contribution. Have the pair also add a picture related to the contribution and realistic details to the stone that make it look authentic. Ask the first three pairs finishing their projects to complete three additional stepping stones, using the information about the weather equipment provided below. Display the resulting 13 paper stones in chronological order on a wall under a banner titled "Stepping Stones to Modern-Day Weather Forecasting."

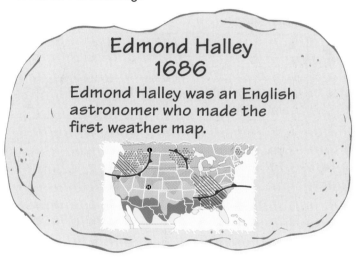

Edmond Halley
1686

Edmond Halley was an English astronomer who made the first weather map.

Scientist	Year	Contribution
Galileo	1593	a type of thermometer
Evangelista Torricelli	1643	barometer
Edmond Halley	1686	weather map
Gabriel Daniel Fahrenheit	1714	mercury thermometer
Anders Celsius	1742	Celsius temperature scale
Horace Bénédict de Saussure	1783	hair hygrometer
Samuel F. B. Morse	1844	perfected the telegraph, which allowed for transmitting weather observations
Vilhelm Bjerknes	1921	explained that changes in weather were due to weather zones called fronts
Lewis Fry Richardson	1922	developed calculations that could be applied to varying atmospheric conditions
John von Neumann	1940s	formulated equations for computers to predict the weather
Equipment		
Radiosondes	1930s	
Radar	1940s	
Weather satellites	1959	

Weather-Wise Survey

Long before meteorologists used weather instruments and computer models, people like fishermen, farmers, and sailors had their own ways of predicting the weather. How? By observing the weather and watching for patterns. To help them remember the patterns, they used sayings and rhymes.

Directions: Help your classmates choose six of the sayings below to use in a survey. Mark the selected sayings with an asterisk (*). Next, survey ten family members or friends to see if they believe these sayings are true. For each selected saying make a tally mark in the true or false column to show how each person responds.

Saying	True	False
The locust sings when it is to be hot and clear.		
Wide black bands on woolly bear caterpillars mean a hard winter is upon us.		
The busier the squirrels, the harder the winter.		
A storm is coming when winter birds are seen to be unusually busy feeding.		
April showers bring May flowers.		
Expect the weather to be fair when crows fly in pairs.		
Red sky at morning, sailors take warning. Red sky at night, sailor's delight.		
A ring around the sun or moon brings rain or snow upon us soon.		
A cow with its tail to the west makes the weather best.		
When dew is on the grass, rain will never come to pass.		
Year of snow, crops will grow.		
If the robin sings in the bush, then the weather will be coarse. If the robin sings on the barn, then the weather will be warm.		
When spiders weave their webs by noon, fine weather is coming soon.		
If bees stay at home, rain will soon come. If they fly away, fine will be the day.		
Swallows fly high, clear blue sky. Swallows fly low, rain we shall know.		
When a squirrel eats nuts in a tree, weather as warm as warm can be.		
A rainbow in the morning is the shepherd's warning. A rainbow at night is the shepherd's delight.		
The higher the cloud, the finer the weather.		
When clouds appear like rocks and towers, the earth's refreshed with frequent showers.		
Wind in the west, weather at its best.		
Clear moon, frost soon.		
When a cow endeavors to scratch its ear, it means a shower is very near. When it thumps its ribs and tail, look out for thunder, lightning, hail.		

©2000 The Education Center, Inc. • *Investigating Science • Weather & Climate* • TEC1732

Breezin' Through a Weather Map

Reading a weather map is a breeze if you use a key to understand its symbols! Use the map shown and its key to answer the questions below.

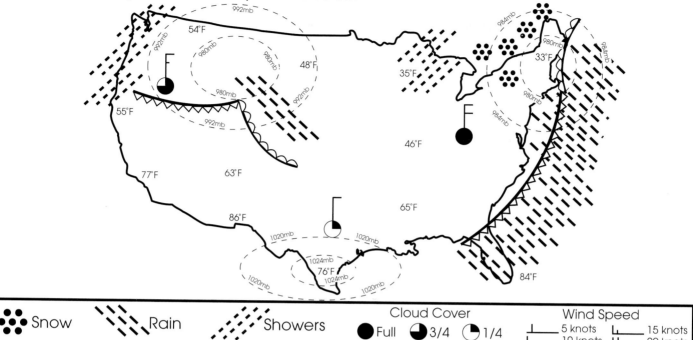

1. Look at the thin dashed lines on the map above. These are *isobars.* They show areas of high and low pressure. Connect each set of dashed isobar lines with a green pencil.

2. Notice that each isobar line connects air-pressure readings of the same number of *millibars* (units of atmospheric pressure) to create a ring. Compare the numbers on each set of rings, beginning with the outermost ring and moving toward the center. If the numbers decrease, write "LOW" in the centermost ring to label it as an area of low pressure. That area could be getting wind or rain. If the numbers increase, write "HIGH" in the centermost ring to label it as an area of high pressure. That area could be having clear weather, unless it's winter. Then it could mean frost or fog.

3. A line of connected triangles indicates a cold front, which can bring lower temperatures, wind, rain, or even snow. Color the triangles of each cold front blue.

4. A line of connected semicircles indicates a warm front, which can bring rising temperatures, rain, or snow. Color the semicircles of the warm front red.

5. Look at the large dots that are either fully or partially shaded in. These dots indicate the amount of cloud cover in an area. Is it cloudier in the eastern half of the United States or the western half?

_____

6. Notice that the large dots have flags attached to them. The flags show the wind speed in each area. Print the wind speed next to each flag. What is the windiest part of the United States: the East, the Northwest, or the South? _____

7. What is the highest wind speed recorded on the map? _____ Where are these winds located?

_____

8. Which part of the United States is getting rain? _____
   Just showers? _____

9. Which part of the United States is getting snow? _____

10. What is the highest temperature recorded on the map? _____ The lowest? _____

©2000 The Education Center, Inc. • *Investigating Science* • *Weather & Climate* • TEC1732 • Key p. 48

Note to the teacher: Use with "Look Who's on the Six O'Clock News!" on page 29. Provide students with green, blue, and red colored pencils to complete this activity. Also provide access to a political map of the United States.

Activity Strips

Announcement: warning **Descriptor:** blizzard conditions expected over the next several hours, with winds of 35 mph or more, falling and drifting snow, and visibility of less than one-fourth mile	**Announcement:** watch **Descriptor:** possibility of tornadoes between 4 P.M. and 6 P.M.
Announcement: watch **Descriptor:** possibility of flooding during the next 12 to 24 hours	**Announcement:** warning **Descriptor:** tornado sighted
Announcement: warning **Descriptor:** overnight temperature expected to fall below 32°F, danger to outdoor plants	**Announcement:** advisory **Descriptor:** be aware that winds could make the temperature feel like −10°F
Announcement: advisory **Descriptor:** be aware that ice expected to accumulate on outdoor surfaces and power lines	**Announcement:** watch **Descriptor:** possibility of heavy snow within the next 36 hours
Announcement: warning **Descriptor:** heavy frost expected, danger to outdoor plants	**Announcement:** warning **Descriptor:** heavy snow expected to begin within the next 12 hours
Announcement: watch **Descriptor:** possibility of winds of 40 mph or more for the next several hours	**Announcement:** warning **Descriptor:** sleet and freezing rain expected within the next 12 hours
Announcement: warning **Descriptor:** heavy rains expected for the next several hours, causing rivers to crest within 12 hours	**Announcement:** watch **Descriptor:** possibility of heavy rains within the next 36 hours
Announcement: watch **Descriptor:** possibility of hurricane conditions within the next 24 to 36 hours	**Announcement:** watch **Descriptor:** possibility of heavy sleet and freezing rain within the next 36 hours
Announcement: warning **Descriptor:** hurricane conditions expected within the next 24 hours	**Announcement:** watch **Descriptor:** possibility of flooding due to melting snow within the next 12 to 24 hours
Announcement: watch **Descriptor:** possibility of severe thunderstorms in the area within the next six hours	**Announcement:** watch **Descriptor:** possibility of coastal flooding within the next 12 to 36 hours due to a tropical storm off the coast
Announcement: warning **Descriptor:** severe thunderstorms with high winds and hail expected for the next hour	**Announcement:** advisory **Descriptor:** be aware that dense fog could continue for the next six hours, with visibility of one-fourth mile or less
Announcement: advisory **Descriptor:** be aware that snow accumulations could range from two to six inches during the next 12 hours	**Announcement:** advisory **Descriptor:** be aware that dangerously high temperatures and humidity levels could continue for the next three days

Note to the teacher: Use with "Warning! Hazardous Weather!" on page 31.

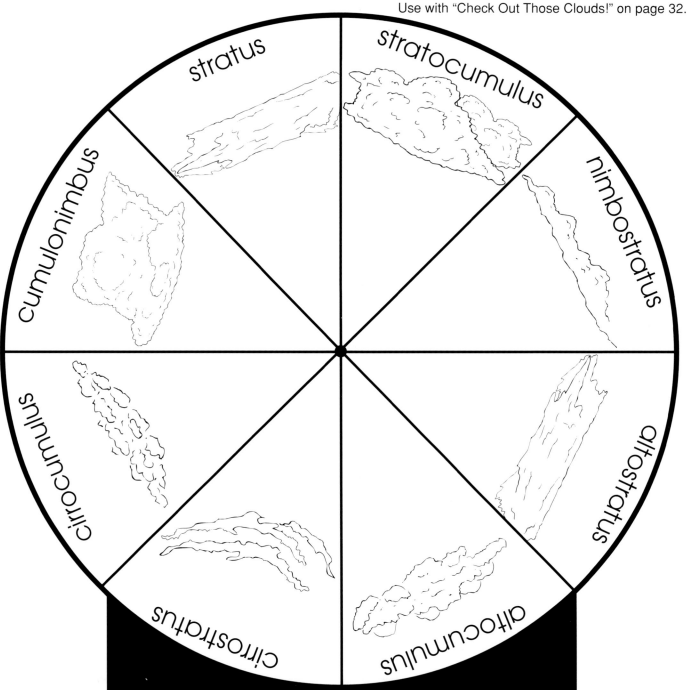

Rules

1. If you spin **stratus, nimbostratus,** or **cumulonimbus,** you should expect precipitation. Move your marker as directed:
   - If you spin **stratus,** you're in a drizzle. Move back one cloud.
   - If you spin **nimbostratus,** you're in snow or rain. Move back two clouds.
   - If you spin **cumulonimbus,** you're in a thunderstorm with heavy rain. Move back three clouds. If you spin **cumulonimbus** two turns in a row, you're in a tornado! Move back to Start.
2. If you spin **any other cloud,** no precipitation is expected. Stay where you are.

Latin Words

alto ("high")

cirro ("curl")

cumulo ("pile")

nimbus ("rain")

stratus ("layered")

Climate

Make climate crystal clear for your students with this collection of activities and ready-to-go reproducibles.

Background for the Teacher

- Climate and weather are different. *Weather* is the condition of the outside air at any given time and place. *Climate* is the average weather in one place over a period of time.
- *Climatologists*—scientists who study climate—mainly rely on temperature and precipitation averages to determine climate.
- Every place on the earth has its own climate.
- Climate is controlled by many factors including latitude, the location of land and water, wind patterns, high and low pressure belts, ocean currents, elevation, landforms, cloud cover, and weather fronts.
- A region's climate affects the kind of clothing people wear, the types of food grown, and the kind of homes lived in.
- Climate also helps determine the types of vegetation and animals that thrive in a particular area.
- Climatologists believe that pollution, which results in the depletion of the ozone layer and an increase in global warming (the greenhouse effect), will cause extreme changes to the earth's climate.

Temperate Reading Topics

Can It Really Rain Frogs? The World's Strangest Weather Events (Spencer Christian's World of Wonders series) by Spencer Christian and Antonia Felix (John Wiley & Sons, Inc.; 1997)

Discovering El Niño: How Fable and Fact Together Help Explain the Weather by Patricia Seibert (The Millbrook Press, Inc.; 1999)

The Greenhouse Effect (Closer Look At series) by Alex Edmonds (Copper Beech Books, 1997)

Volcanoes (Closer Look At series) by Jen Green (Copper Beech Books, 1998)

Weather Explained: A Beginner's Guide to the Elements (Your World Explained series) by Derek M. Elsom (Henry Holt and Company, 1997)

Vacation Variations
(Identifying State Climate Trends, Statistics)

Use this creative activity to teach your students about the climate characteristics of different states. Begin by explaining to students how climate and weather are different (see the background information on this page). Then, with students' help, make a list of words that describe the climate of different states (for example, Arizona—hot, dry, sunny; Hawaii—hot, wet). Pair students and give each pair an almanac, markers or crayons, and a copy of page 44. Assign every pair a different state to research. Have the pair use the almanac to locate and graph its state's average monthly temperatures and precipitation levels in the space provided on the reproducible. Next, display a copy of the mean, median, mode, and range information shown. Direct the pair to use the information from its bar graphs on page 44 to fill in the blanks about the yearly mean, median, mode, and range for its state. Finally, point out to students that vacationers want to know about a state's climate—the average temperature, high and low temperatures, and average precipitation amounts—to help them determine when to travel and what to pack. Have each pair draw conclusions about its state's climate (for example, parts of Utah have a cold, wet climate in January—perfect for a ski trip) and present the information to the class. Bon voyage!

Mean: Add the set of numbers together. Then divide the sum by the number of items in the set.

Median: Arrange the numbers in the set from least to greatest. Then identify the middle number. (For a set with an even number of items, identify the *two* middle numbers. Add those two numbers together and then divide the sum by two.)

Mode: Identify the number that appears most often in a set of numbers. Some sets of numbers do not have a mode.

Range: Subtract the least number in the set from the greatest number.

It's All in Your Latitude
(Demonstration)

Introduce your students to one of nature's most important climate controls—latitude. To begin, explain that the sun's rays strike the earth at different angles because of the earth's tilt. Emphasize that land areas nearest the equator generally receive the most direct sunlight, so these areas have higher temperatures. Land areas farther away from the equator receive less direct sunlight, so these areas have lower temperatures. Then demonstrate how the angle of the sun's rays affects land temperature by gathering the materials listed and following the directions below.

Materials: desk lamp (similar to the one shown), 2 outdoor thermometers, 9" x 13" clear baking dish filled with sand or dirt

Directions:

1. Place the pan of dirt where every student can see it. Place one thermometer in the dirt at each end of the pan. Make sure both thermometers are facing forward.
2. Place the lamp near the first thermometer so that the light is shining directly on it as shown.
3. Observe the thermometers for about 20 minutes. At five-minute intervals, choose a different student to read and record the temperatures on chart paper.
4. Finally, discuss with students how the thermometer nearer the lamp became warmer than the thermometer farther away. Point out to students that this is similar to the way land nearer the equator receives more of the sun's energy than the land farther away.

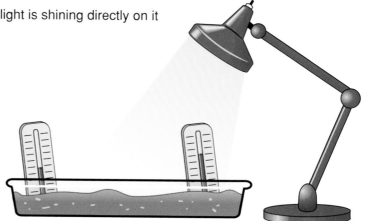

Location, Location, Location
(Map Skills, Identifying Climatic Areas)

Use this map activity to activate your students' critical-thinking skills about different climates and places on earth. Begin by reminding students that there is a relationship between climate and location on the earth's surface. Because the earth is tilted, the sun's rays strike it at different angles, causing lands closer to the equator to be warmer and lands farther from the equator to be cooler. Explain that scientists divide the earth into six major regions, called *biomes,* based on climate and plant and animal life. Next, distribute a copy of page 45 and crayons to each student. Instruct the student to listen as you read each biome clue below. Call on one student to explain the location of the biome based on the information in the clue; then direct each student to label his key and then color in the correct biome on the map. After all the biomes are colored in, pair students and have each partner make up biome clues of his own. Have the partners test each other's biome knowledge by reading the clues and determining the biome being described.

Biome Clues

I can be found in the coldest parts of the world. I am usually covered with snow. There are long winters and short, cool summers here. Because I am found in the most northern areas, it is too cool for trees to grow here. *I am the tundra.*

I am considered a subarctic forest. Trees can grow here even though I am located in the north and it is very cold. I begin where the tundra ends. *I am the taiga.*

I have a seasonal climate where there are warm summers and cold winters. My climate allows deciduous trees (trees that shed their leaves seasonally) and evergreen trees (trees that keep their leaves all year) to grow. I can be found across most of the eastern United States. *I am the temperate forest.*

I have a warm, wet climate. My climate supports a large variety of plant and animal life. I can be found in a large section of northern South America. *I am the tropical rain forest.*

I am usually located between deserts and humid, forest-covered areas. There are two types of me: *steppes,* which have short grasses, and *prairies,* which have tall grasses. I am found on six of the seven continents. *I am the grassland.*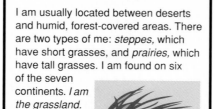

I am a hot, empty, dry region. Even though there is little rainfall where I am located, plants like cacti thrive in my climate. My largest area is in the Sahara in northern Africa. *I am the desert.*

A Climate Moderator
(Demonstration)

Can two locations found along the same latitude have different climates? Certainly, when proximity to the ocean or another large body of water is considered. Explain to students that coastal regions experience less temperature variation than inland areas because they are nearer water, which heats and cools more slowly than land. The farther an inland area is from a large body of water, the greater its annual temperature range. Display a world map or globe for students to see. Point out to students an inland city and a coastal city at about the same latitude, such as Boston, Massachusetts, and Omaha, Nebraska. Explain that on average Omaha has cooler January and warmer July temperatures than Boston because Omaha is farther inland. Then show your students how water can act as a climate moderator by collecting the materials listed and following the directions below. As a follow-up activity, pair students and have each pair research the climates of two locations with similar latitudes: one near a large body of water and one farther inland. Have each pair share its findings with the class.

Materials for demonstration:
2 metal loaf pans, 2 outdoor thermometers, soil, plastic wrap, tape

Directions:
1. Fill one loaf pan three-fourths full of soil. Fill the other loaf pan three-fourths full of water.
2. Tape a thermometer on the inside of each pan as shown.
3. Cover each pan with plastic wrap.
4. Place the pans in the shade. Record the temperatures of each pan after one minute.
5. Place the pans in a sunny spot. Record the rise in temperature after five minutes.
6. Move the pans back into the shade and observe how the temperature of the pan filled with soil falls more quickly.

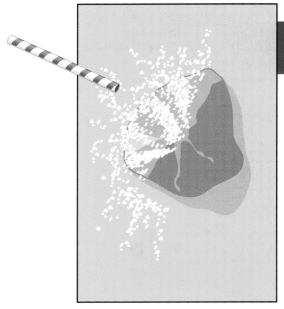

Elevation Station
(Making a Model, Observation)

Heighten your students' awareness of the role mountains play in controlling climate with this hands-on activity. Begin by explaining to students that mountains affect air movements and precipitation patterns. When air reaches a mountain, it will rise and cool. The moisture in the air is released as precipitation on the *windward side* of the mountain. After the air has lost most of its precipitation, it passes over the mountain. Because of this, the *leeward side* of the mountain—the side away from the wind—is drier than the windward side and often has less vegetation. Give your students an opportunity to witness how a mountain can control climate—and the natural vegetation and animals that thrive in a mountain area—with the following activity. Divide your class into groups; then provide each group with the materials listed below and a copy of the directions shown.

Materials for each group: newspaper, one 12" x 18" sheet of construction paper, clay, $\frac{1}{2}$ c. of powdered sugar in a tall drinking glass, 1 straw for each member

Directions:
1. Spread several sheets of newspaper on a desk or table.
2. Use the clay to form a mountain two to three inches high on the construction paper.
3. Each member places his finger over one end of the straw and then takes turns placing the other end in the powdered sugar.
4. While eye level with the desk or table, take turns blowing the powdered sugar gently onto one side of the mountain.
5. Observe the sugar patterns on the mountain. Notice how the windward side of the mountain (the side facing you) received more precipitation (sugar) than the leeward side.

What a Blast!
(Research, Writing)

Highlight the effects of volcanoes on the earth's climate with this research activity that's sure to be a blast! Begin by explaining to students that a volcanic eruption can send large amounts of dust, ash, and gases into the atmosphere. This dust can stay suspended in the air for years, limiting the amount of sunlight that reaches the earth. Share with students that the eruption of Mount Pinatubo in the Philippines in 1991 sent 15 million tons of dust and gases into the atmosphere. Within a year, the dust had spread out across the earth, causing the average temperature to fall 0.9°F, resulting in cooler summers and harsher winters. Have students research other important volcanic eruptions and their climatic effects. Pair students and assign each pair an eruption from the list shown. Have the pair use encyclopedias and other resource materials (see literature list on page 38) to research the eruption and record any climatic changes, such as changes in atmospheric or agricultural conditions. Then have the pair record its information on a colorful construction paper cutout of an erupting volcano as shown. Set aside time for the partners to share their findings with the class. Display the volcanoes chronologically on a bulletin board titled "What a Blast!"

Important Eruptions
Vesuvius (Italy, A.D. 79)
Mount Etna (Sicily, 1669)
Mount Tambora (Indonesia, 1815)
Mauna Loa (Hawaii, 1855–1856)
Krakatau (Indonesia, 1883)
Cotopaxi (Ecuador, 1877)
Mont Pelée (Martinique, 1902)
Paricutín (Mexico, 1943)
Mount St. Helens (Washington, 1980)
El Chichón (Mexico, 1982)
Nevado del Ruiz (Colombia, 1985)

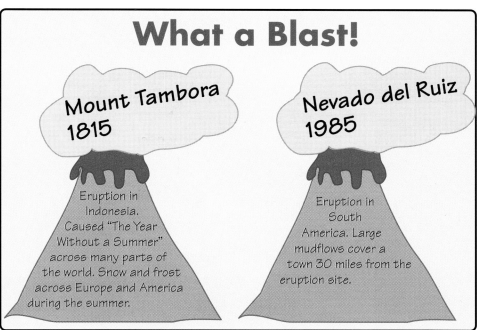

What a Blast!

Mount Tambora 1815
Eruption in Indonesia. Caused "The Year Without a Summer" across many parts of the world. Snow and frost across Europe and America during the summer.

Nevado del Ruiz 1985
Eruption in South America. Large mudflows cover a town 30 miles from the eruption site.

The Atmosphere

400 miles above sea level
thermosphere
50–55 miles above sea level
mesosphere
30 miles above sea level
OZONE LAYER
stratosphere
7.5 miles above sea level
troposphere

Ozone Action
(Research, Writing)

Motivate your students to become more involved in preserving the ozone layer, thus protecting themselves and the earth, with this activity. Use a copy of the diagram shown to help explain to students how a thinning of the ozone layer would affect the earth's climate. Point out to students that the ozone layer, located in the earth's stratosphere, protects life on the earth by shielding us from some of the sun's ultraviolet rays. If the hole in the ozone grows, it could cause more cases of skin cancer and eye disorders in humans, and it could damage the marine food chain by killing plants and then the animals that eat them. Have students use various resource materials to research facts about the hole in the ozone layer. Then allow each student to make a poster, pamphlet, or flyer describing the hazards of ozone depletion and the steps we can take to protect ourselves from the sun's harmful rays. Hold an Ozone Layer Awareness Rally by displaying the students' posters around your classroom and inviting students from other classes to come and learn about its importance.

Helping Global Warming Hit Home
(Reading for Information)

Create a climate of conservation for your students with this activity that focuses on the effects of global warming. To begin, make a copy of the informative paragraph shown below for each student. As a class, read aloud the paragraph and discuss the effects of global warming on the earth. Next, with students' help, list ways to stop global warming and cut down on the amount of carbon dioxide in the air (for example, use less electricity, walk instead of drive, and recycle). Then give each student a copy of the checklist on the top of page 46. Instruct the student to take the checklist home to complete with an adult's assistance. When the child returns the checklist and has signed the contract at the bottom of the form, present him with a copy of the award on the bottom of page 46.

Live in a Green House

Reduce the amount of carbon dioxide your family contributes to the earth's atmosphere. Take this page home and complete the checklist. (Ask an adult for help.) On the line next to each item, write a sentence describing actions you took or observations you made. Use the back of this page if you need more space. Then fill out the contract below and return this page to your teacher.

✔ 1. Run the dishwasher only if it's full; then dry the dishes using the energy-saving setting. _I waited to run the dishes until my sister was done making cookies._

✔ 2. Use warm or cold water to wash clothes, not hot. _We used cold water when we washed clothes._

✔ 3. Make sure your water heater's thermostat is set at 120°F. _My Dad helped me check the hot water heater._

___ 4. Stop overcooling or overheating your house. Adjust your thermostat a few degrees lower in the winter and a few degrees higher in the summer. _____

___ 5. Use energy-efficient lightbulbs. _____

___ 6. Take shorter showers or use less hot water. _____

___ 7. Walk, bike, or carpool. _____

___ 8. Buy products that have less packaging and are made from reusable materials. _____

___ 9. Plant a tree or shrub to help reduce carbon dioxide in the air. _____

___ 10. Recycle! _____

I, _James_ , will try to prevent global warming by reducing the amount of
   name
carbon dioxide that my family and I send into the earth's atmosphere every day.

Student's Signature _____ Date _____

What Goes Up Doesn't Come Down

Climatologists are concerned about how the climate will change if the earth continues to warm up. Over the past 140 years, the earth has warmed about 1.1°F due to a growing population and the burning of *fossil fuels,* such as coal, oil, and gas. Burning fossil fuels releases gases into the atmosphere called *greenhouse gases.* Sunlight can pass through these gases, but the heat from the surface of the earth becomes trapped by them, causing the earth's average temperature to become warmer. *Carbon dioxide* gas is responsible for about half of the global warming in the past 140 years. Humans increase carbon dioxide in the air by burning fossil fuels in cars, factories, and homes, and by cutting down and burning the rain forests. If the temperatures on earth continue to rise, it is possible that there could be rising sea levels, an increase in desert land, and a reduction in the amount of food produced on the earth.

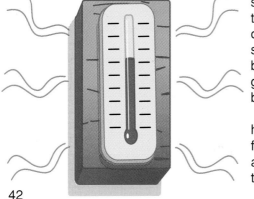

City Heat, Country Cool
(Experiment, Critical Thinking)

Why might the city be warmer than the surrounding country in the summertime? Motivate your students to use scientific thinking to find the answer to this real-life question! Ahead of time gather two outdoor thermometers, a brick, and a section of sod (purchased from a gardening center or carefully removed from a lawn). Divide students into small groups. Have each group write on a sheet of paper a reason or hypothesis explaining the answer to the question above. Together with students, take the brick and sod square outside to a bright, sunny area. Place one thermometer on the brick (representing the city) and the other thermometer on the sod square (representing the country). Have each group record the temperatures. After an hour have each group record the two new temperatures of the brick and sod square. Then bring the brick and the sod square inside. Review the temperatures over a ten-minute period, checking them every minute. After a marked change in temperature, give each group the opportunity to modify its hypothesis. Then explain to students that most of the sun's energy that reaches the earth is used to evaporate water. Materials like brick don't absorb water, so the sun's energy causes it to retain heat. Plants, grass, and other natural areas receive the same amount of energy from the sun, but are cooled by the water evaporating from their leaves.

Follow up this activity by having each group consider why the pavement is hot, but the grass is cool on your toes in the summertime. Have the groups list factors that might make a pavement warmer, such as buildings that surround it and prevent wind from blowing the heat away, and heat from vehicles warming the air around the pavement.

Climate Collage
(Art, Research, Critical Thinking)

Use this colorful art activity to teach your students how climate affects people's lives no matter where they live. Begin by covering a bulletin board with light-colored paper and titling it "Climate Collage." Divide the board into four sections and write one of the following topics at the top of each section: *clothing, food, shelter,* and *transportation.* Explain to students that climate influences the types of clothing people wear, the foods they grow, the homes they build, and the transportation they use. Group students; then assign each group one topic from the bulletin board. Provide the group with magazines, newspapers, encyclopedias, and other research materials. Direct each group to research the effects climate has on its topic. Next, have the group cut out pictures of its topic from the magazines and newspapers. Instruct the group members to make a collage by gluing the pictures on their section of the bulletin board and writing a caption explaining which climate the picture might be found in as shown. As a follow-up activity, make a copy of the reproducible on page 47 for each student to complete as directed.

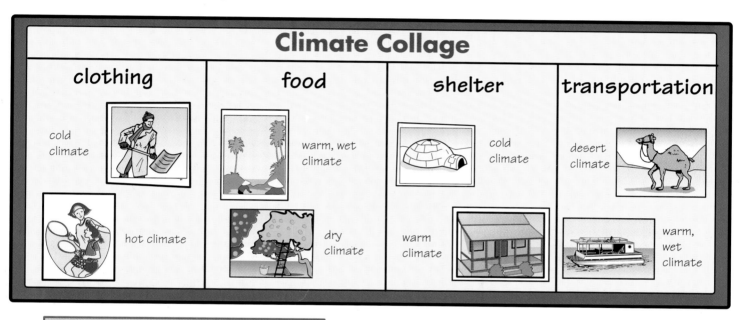

Climate Collage

clothing	food	shelter	transportation

clothing — cold climate, hot climate
food — warm, wet climate, dry climate
shelter — cold climate, warm climate
transportation — desert climate, warm, wet climate

El Niño
by Tim and José

Fiction   Fact

Crazy Climatic Changes
(Research, Writing)

Need a fantastic way to conclude your climate unit? Get your students fired up about climatic phenomena with this researching and writing activity. Explain to students that when an area's climate changes for a short period of time, it is called a *season*. Sometimes climate changes last longer or shorter than a season. Give students an opportunity to research some well-known climatic events, such as El Niño, La Niña, drought, Indian summer, northers, floods, and doldrums. Pair students and assign each pair an event to research using encyclopedias and other research materials. Have each pair begin by collaborating to write a myth, legend, or simple description that attempts to explain its event. Then have the pair research and summarize the scientific facts about its climatic event. Next, direct each pair to glue its story and facts to a sheet of 12" x 18" construction paper and label and illustrate it as shown. Finally, invite the pair to share its climatic phenomena fact and fiction with the class.

Keeping Up With Climate

Climatologists—scientists who study climate—use temperature and precipitation averages to determine climate. Use an almanac to find out your assigned state's average temperature and precipitation for each month of the year. Then follow the steps below to complete each graph.

A. Create a bar graph to show your state's average monthly temperatures. Label the vertical axis with a range of numbers that will include the lowest and highest average temperatures of the year. Complete the graph by coloring each month's bar a different color.

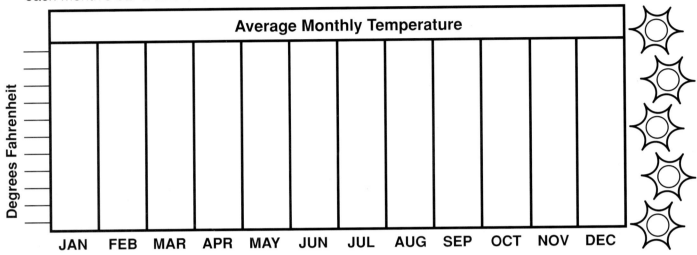

B. Create a pictograph to show your state's average monthly precipitation. Using the key, determine the number of symbols needed for each month.

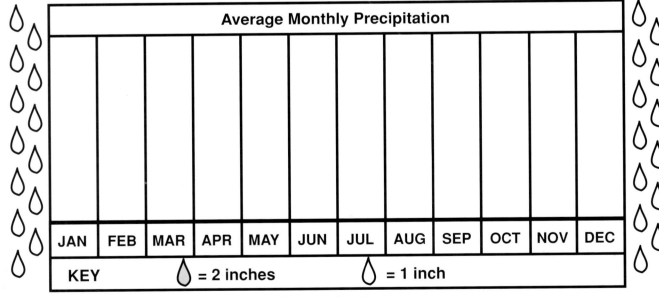

C. Use the information from the graphs to fill in the blanks below.

	Yearly Temperature		Yearly Precipitation
mean	_____	mean	_____
median	_____	median	_____
mode	_____	mode	_____
range	_____	range	_____

Get Acclimatized*

The earth is divided into six major land regions called *biomes*. Each region's climate is different. The differences in climate affect the kind of plant and animal life found in each region. Listen as your teacher reads each biome clue; then label the key and color the correct area(s) on the map.

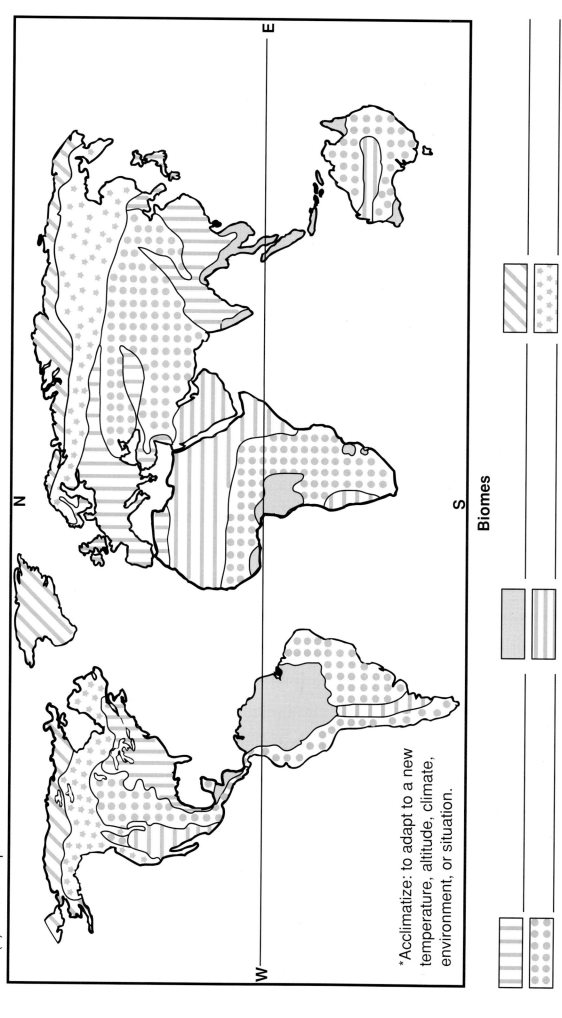

Biomes

*Acclimatize: to adapt to a new temperature, altitude, climate, environment, or situation.

©2000 The Education Center, Inc. • *Investigating Science • Weather & Climate* • TEC1732 • Key p. 48

Note to the teacher: Use with "Location, Location, Location" on page 39.

45

Live in a Green House

Reduce the amount of carbon dioxide your family contributes to the earth's atmosphere. Take this page home and complete the checklist. (Ask an adult for help.) On the line next to each item, write a sentence describing actions you took or observations you made. Use the back of this page if you need more space. Then fill out the contract below and return this page to your teacher.

____1. Run the dishwasher only if it's full; then dry the dishes using the energy-saving setting.
_____

____2. Use warm or cold water to wash clothes, not hot._____

____3. Make sure your water heater's thermostat is set at 120°F._____
_____

____4. Stop overcooling or overheating your house. Adjust your thermostat a few degrees lower in the winter and a few degrees higher in the summer._____
_____

____5. Use energy-efficient lightbulbs._____

____6. Take shorter showers or use less hot water._____

____7. Walk, bike, or carpool._____

____8. Buy products that have less packaging and are made from reusable materials._____
_____

____9. Plant a tree or shrub to help reduce carbon dioxide in the air._____
_____

___10. Recycle! _____

I, _____, will try to prevent global warming by reducing the amount of
   name

carbon dioxide that my family and I send into the earth's atmosphere every day.

Student's Signature _____ Date _____

Keep It Green!

_____
is awarded this Keep It Green award
for successfully completing the Live in a *Green* House checklist.

Teacher's Signature _____ Date _____

Virtual Visiting

Imagine you get to visit a family in each of the different locations below. Use encyclopedias or other reference materials to research the climate of each location; then write information describing each place on the blanks provided.

Tahiti

Location: _____

Climate: _____

Types of shelter and food you might find:

_____

Kinds of clothing you might wear: _____

_____

Swiss Alps

Location: _____

Climate: _____

Types of shelter and food you might find:

_____

Kinds of clothing you might wear: _____

_____

Sahara

Location: _____

Climate: _____

Types of shelter and food you might find:

_____

Kinds of clothing you might wear: _____

_____

Rome

Location: _____

Climate: _____

Types of shelter and food you might find:

_____

Kinds of clothing you might wear: _____

_____

Amazon

Location: _____

Climate: _____

Types of shelter and food you might find:

_____

Kinds of clothing you might wear: _____

_____

SIBERIA

Location: _____

Climate: _____

Types of shelter and food you might find:

_____

Kinds of clothing you might wear: _____

_____

Mount McKinley

Location: _____

Climate: _____

Types of shelter and food you might find:

_____

Kinds of clothing you might wear: _____

_____

Tucson

Location: _____

Climate: _____

Types of shelter and food you might find:

_____

Kinds of clothing you might wear: _____

_____

Answer Keys

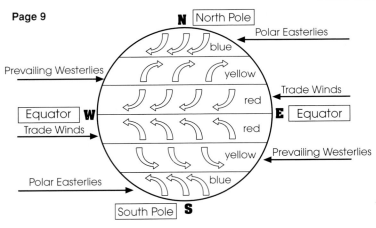

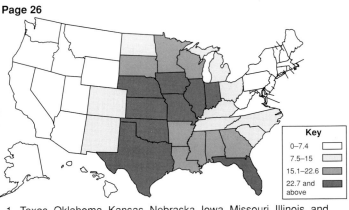

Page 9

Bonus Box answer: Coriolis force

Page 15
(Students' definitions may vary.)

2. Cumulonimbus — heap + rain — Cumulonimbus clouds are large, fluffy storm clouds.

3. Altocumulus — higher + heap — Altocumulus clouds are heaps of clouds seen higher in the sky.

4. Nimbostratus — rain + spread out — Nimbostratus clouds are thick rain clouds spread across the sky.

5. Cirrostratus — curl + spread out — Cirrostratus clouds are curls of high clouds spread out across the sky.

6. Altostratus — higher + spread out — Altostratus clouds are higher, thick clouds spread out across the sky.

7. Stratocumulus — spread out + heap — Stratocumulus clouds are puffy clouds spread out across the sky.

Page 24
Beaufort Scale 0—It's so calm. It feels like there is no wind at all.
Beaufort Scale 1—The smoke from that chimney is slowly blowing toward the north.
Beaufort Scale 2—The light breeze feels nice and cool.
Beaufort Scale 3—The leaves in that yard are being blown around.
Beaufort Scale 5—That small maple tree is swaying gently.
Beaufort Scale 6—You may need a stronger umbrella; the winds are 29 MPH!
Beaufort Scale 7—That whole tree is moving in the 34-MPH wind.
Beaufort Scale 8—Some of the twigs are breaking off of that tree.
Beaufort Scale 9—That house just lost three shingles from its roof!
Beaufort Scale 10—That tree just pulled right out of the ground!
Beaufort Scale 11—The storm's winds are up to 69 MPH and are causing a lot of damage!
Beaufort Scale 12–17—Evacuate immediately! The winds are over 80 MPH!

Page 25
Students' answers will vary. Possible answers are listed.
1. the Bahamas
2. Puerto Rico, because Windy was much closer to it than to the Dominican Republic
3. the prevailing westerlies
4. Students' answers will vary. Answers should include that Florida was in some danger, but people would probably not have been made to evacuate until there was more of a threat.

Page 27
1. 113.2 inches
2. 43 days
3. 90 inches
4. the tornado in Texas, 106–111 MPH
5. largest hailstone, 30 years ago
6. 101–106 MPH greater

Page 26

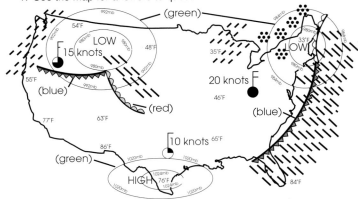

1. Texas, Oklahoma, Kansas, Nebraska, Iowa, Missouri, Illinois, and Indiana. Students' answers will vary, but should include that these states have the highest number of tornadoes and are close to each other in location.
2. Florida
3. Students' responses will vary, but should include that the states in Tornado Alley are plains states. This is good for tornadoes, which move most easily over flat, open spaces.

Page 35
1. See the map for answers to questions 1–4.

5. the eastern half
6. See the map for the labeling of wind speeds. It is windiest in the East.
7. The highest wind speed is 20 knots. These winds are in the Ohio-Kentucky-West Virginia area, southwest of a low-pressure area.
8. The area north of the Great Plains and all of the east coast are getting rain. The northwest coast and the Great Lakes area are getting showers.
9. The western parts of the Northeast are getting snow.
10. The highest temperature is 86°F. The lowest temperature is 33°F.

Page 45

Page 47
Students' answers for "types of shelter and food you might find" and "kinds of clothing you might wear" will vary. Accept reasonable answers.
Tahiti—South Pacific island, tropical climate
Sahara—North Africa, desert climate
Amazon—South America, tropical rain forest climate
Mount McKinley—Alaska, cold climate
Swiss Alps—Switzerland, cold climate
Rome—Italy, mild climate
Siberia—Russia, frigid climate
Tucson—Arizona, warm and sunny climate